From PASSION TO PROFIT

Start Your Business in 6 Weeks or Less!

A step-by-step guide to making money from your hobby by selling online

Claire Hughes

David and Charles

www.stitchcraftcreate.co.uk

CONTENTS

✦ INTRODUCTION ✦

These days, everyone can be an entrepreneur! You no longer need a fat savings account, a rich benefactor or an angel investor to start a business doing what you love. Thanks to the Internet, it's never been easier to make money by sharing your passion with the world. But all the options can seem confusing and overwhelming if you're not a technical whiz or have never owned a business before.

Perhaps you've thought about starting something in the past but never quite got it off the ground? Maybe you've been talking about an idea with friends but haven't quite found the right time (or courage) to start? Perhaps you've been selling in the 'real world' and want to make the jump to doing this online? Or maybe this is the first time you've ever given serious consideration to starting a business? Whatever your story, now is your time to start!

Over the next six weeks I'm going to be your guide as we work our way through the step-by-step process of getting your creative business out of your head and onto the World Wide Web.

Start a business in six weeks or less – are you completely mad?

Isn't it crazy to put that extra time pressure on yourself? Isn't starting a business hard enough? So let me explain the reason I designed the step-by-step course outlined in this book to run over six weeks. Have you ever started a project that just went on, and on, and on, and...well, you get the idea. In my experience (and please forgive the generalization) creative people are often perfectionists who like to tinker with things until they're just so.

For example, the first time I decided to start a business I spent weeks trying to find the perfect logo and 'researching' competitors online. Yet I completely avoided all the important things like actually defining what I was going to offer and thinking about where I was going to find customers, because – let's be honest – I was a little bit scared. Needless to say, that business never really got off the ground. By the time I'd found the perfect logo, I'd run out of steam. Eventually friends and family stopped asking what was happening with my business, and I stopped having to mumble excuses.

I don't want the same thing to happen to you. I want you to experience the thrill and satisfaction of launching your own business, and of doing something for yourself. So by setting a deadline, I'm giving you a workable target to to aim for. By working through the course content week by week, as many students have done since I first started teaching this course, I'm hoping you'll build up a sense of momentum without becoming overwhelmed.

Last but not least, for most people with a day job or other commitments, six weeks is a manageable amount of time. It's challenging, but realistic. It's also just short enough that your friends/husband/dog/kids will forgive you for abandoning them when you get out the other side.

What can I expect when I get to the end of the book?

A (virtual) round of applause and a celebratory hug! If you work through the materials, complete the worksheets and carry out all the actions recommended week by week, you should be ready to launch your website or online shop in six weeks. Will it be perfect? Will you be 100 per cent happy with it? Should you ring up your boss and quit your day job? Of course not! But you'll have something tangible to show the world, and a solid foundation from which to grow your creative business.

How can I make the most of this book?

Each week, read through the week introduction first to get an idea of the tasks you'll need to complete. Then set aside some time to read through the materials and complete the worksheets, as well as any additional research or actions that are suggested. Depending on the stage you're at, this might include taking photographs of products you want to sell, researching the best legal structure for your business or adding service descriptions to your online shop. The key is to plan ahead. You'll find there are lots of useful resources at the back of the book, which you'll want to refer to throughout. These include blogs and websites aimed at the creative community, which can be a brilliant source of additional help and support.

Try to remember

Sometimes there isn't such a thing as a right or wrong answer. Often when you're running a business, you just have to try things and see what works for you. This will occasionally mean stepping outside of your comfort zone! If in doubt, ask yourself: 'What's the worst that could happen?' There are very few things at this stage in your business that can't be un-done. So just get started and have fun.

WHAT CREATIVE BUSINESS DO I WANT?

Week One

Welcome to Week One! This week we're going to be focusing on YOU. Your interests, your ambitions, your skills and what you want to get out of having a creative business of your very own.

I'll be asking you to start thinking about products and services you might like to sell, and generally giving your entrepreneurial brain a good dusting down.

Are you excited yet? Great! Let's get started.

WEEK One

SET YOUR INTENTION

So you've made the decision to start a creative business, bought (or borrowed) this book and are ready to dive in. Congratulations! First, I'd like to ask you an important question: What sort of business do you actually want to have?

Not just so you have a vision of what you want to achieve. But to become clear in your own mind about what you would like your day-to-day experience of running a business to be like.

Why is this so important?

- When you haven't spent time thinking about the type of business you ultimately want to have, it's easy to be pulled in lots of different directions when the orders start rolling in. This can make it hard to focus and know what to do first
- Just going with the flow can be great. But it can also take you down the wrong path, and lead to the development of a business you don't even like. If you're constantly saying 'yes' to opportunities because you're afraid to turn them down, you could be on a fast track to business owner burn out

I've seen too many lovely, creative people turn a hobby into a business but then end up completely over worked and stressed. Why? Because they weren't completely clear about what they wanted BEFORE their business took off.

Think of it this way. Would you get into a car and start driving without a destination in mind? Maybe, if you were out for a relaxing Sunday afternoon spin. But most times when you get into a car and drive, it's because you want to get somewhere. The fact you have a destination in mind means you know which roads to take (and which to avoid). You know roughly how much fuel you'll need to get there, and who to take along for the ride.

It's not just the destination we want to think about though, but also the journey. What do you want that to be like? Who do you want with you in that car? Do you want a co-pilot, or would you rather travel alone? Will you be driving at full throttle the whole way, or adopting a more leisurely pace? Will you be driving in a shiny new Ferrari, or a vintage camper van?

It's easy to follow someone else's map when you start your creative business, but that can only get you so far. You need to spend some time thinking about WHY you want to start a business and WHAT you want your business to be like. And there's no better time to do that than now.

Imagine your dream business

WORKSHEET

The aim of the following worksheet is to help you set your intention and work out what type of business you actually want to create, which will help you answer a lot of questions like:

- What product or service should I sell?
- Should I run my own website or a marketplace shop?
- How much should I charge for my products?

We will cover the answers to all these questions later in this book. You'll find we refer back to your answers from this worksheet lots of times as you progress through the six week course, so if you're tempted to skip it don't!

Use this exercise to become excited about your dream business!

At the very least, this exercise will get you excited about having a creative business that you love. This will give you a dose of much-needed motivation to get you started, and will also prove useful for you to refer back to when those 'Aargh, what am I doing this for?' niggles crop up.

Are you ready to get started? Make a cup of tea (or pour yourself a glass of wine), set aside some quiet time when you won't be interrupted and let's dive in!

It's time to get into your time machine. Imagine that your business has been up and running for approximately two-and-a-half years. You're out of the start-up phase, your business is established, and you're generally happy with the way things are going.

Now answer the following questions from this place in time. There are no right or wrong answers; this is your DREAM business. You're getting your creative juices flowing and imagining what this business could be like.

1. **What tasks and activities are you doing on a day-to-day basis?**

2. **What are you NOT doing?**

3. **How much time are you spending working on your business each week?**

4. **How much money are you making?**

5. **What types of products and services are you offering?**

6. What price ranges are you selling at?

7. Who are your best customers, and what do they come to you for?

8. How many orders are you handling every week?

9. Who are you working with: are you alone, or part of a team?

10. Who is talking and writing about your business, and what are they saying?

11. Where are you working: from home, a studio, or somewhere else?

12. It's Friday afternoon at the end of a busy week: how do you feel?

Take time to read through your answers. Are you surprised by what you have written? You'll refer back to your answers again and again over the next six weeks – and beyond!

CREATE A VISION BOARD

If you're anything like me and the creative people I work with on a day-to-day basis, visuals float your boat! So when you have filled out your dream business worksheet (see Imagine Your Dream Business Worksheet), why not have a go at creating a vision board for your business?

What is a vision board?

A vision board is basically a board (or a sheet of paper) that contains images and words to represent whatever you want to be, to do or to have in your business or life.

How can a vision board help me start a business?

Some people scoff at vision boards and the like, dismissing them as hippy-dippy, new age rubbish. But I think they're great! Creating a vision board can really help you with the following things:

Get clear on what you want

Creating a vision board can help anchor your dream business in your subconscious mind, basically helping it to sink in. Even if you don't believe in the Law of Attraction, manifestation or any of that stuff, I believe that good things will happen to you when you become clear about what you want from your business. It's like you're making a declaration to the universe and to yourself, and doing this visually really seems to help.

Give you a motivation boost

Looking at your vision board can remind you why you decided to start a business, and can help keep you focused on the bigger picture on those darker days when technology and spread sheets are driving you round the bend. Plus, it's fun! Who doesn't like getting creative with scissors and glue? I know I do!

How do I create a vision board?

Now that we're living in the digital age, there are two ways to create a vision board: the old school way, and the new school way. Both are fun, so just see what appeals to you. To get started with either one, first read through the answers you wrote down on the dream business worksheet (see Imagine Your Dream Business Worksheet) so they are fresh in your mind.

Old school vision board

Start by gathering old magazines, newspapers and brochures – anything that might contain images to represent aspects of your dream business – then use them to cut out images, words and anything you would like to stick on your vision board. Glue these items onto your board along with glitter, paint or photographs; basically anything that inspires you and helps you to think about the dream business you really want to create. You might want to add keywords that you'd like to associate with your business, and maybe even a photo or drawing of yourself.

New school vision board

These days it's really easy to create an entirely digital vision board, too. I love to use Pinterest (www.pinterest.com), an online pinboard tool that is completely free to use. To create your vision board on Pinterest, just create a new board (you can choose to keep it secret if you want), then 'pin' on it images, quotes and videos from websites that appeal to you. The great thing about using Pinterest for this is that you don't need physical space to create or store your vision board. Plus, thanks to the wonders of the Internet, you'll have an endless supply of images to work with, rather than being restricted by your stock of magazines!

Where do I keep my vision board?

Once you've created your vision board, it's up to you what you do with it. You might want to stick it on the wall above your desk, so you can look at it every day. Or maybe you feel a bit shy about having it where other people can see, so would rather keep it somewhere you can bring it out when you want to be reminded of it. If you've created your vision board on Pinterest, you can keep it secret so only you can find the link and see what you have added to it; or you can choose to make it public so other people can look at it, too.

Whatever you decide to do with your vision board, have fun!

IDENTIFY YOUR PASSIONS & SKILLS

Now that you've thought about what you want your business to be like, it's time to start thinking about the personal assets you'll need to get your venture off the ground.

By personal assets, I don't mean money or equipment at this stage. I'm talking about something much more important and exciting than that; those really, really important assets you have as a creative person and fledgling entrepreneur. These are your PASSIONS and your SKILLS.

Whatever it is, if you love doing something and are equally passionate about sharing this with others, that's a great start!

Why your passions give you a head start

Starting a business based on a hobby or interest can be a real advantage. First, this is because building a business based on something you really enjoy should make it a lot more fun! Secondly though, being passionate about the product or service you plan to sell will give you an important competitive edge. If you're genuinely passionate about your business rather than just doing it for the money, customers will pick up on that. Your passion will shine through and help you to connect with potential customers, which will lead to more sales. Excellent!

If you're reading this book, the chances are that you already have a hobby or interest that you really enjoy. Perhaps you have a few potential business ideas in mind? Maybe your stash of vintage materials is getting out of hand, and you're thinking about starting an online fabric shop? Maybe you're a dab hand at crochet, and have been making items for friends and family for years? Or maybe your passion is drawing or making cards?

Understand 'doing' skills versus 'business' skills

It's often said that, as a creative business owner and entrepreneur, you need to be three different people at once:

1. **The Technician:** the person who does the actual job of making and delivering the product or service to customers.

2. **The Manager:** the planner and organizer who keeps things running smoothly and puts the right systems in place.

3. **The Entrepreneur:** the strategist who's always driving the business forward and looking ahead.

It's really tempting to think you only need the 'doing' or technical skills when starting a business based on your hobby. But it's important to think about the other skills you might need too, as they are usually pretty different. To give you an example, take a look at these tables for some examples of 'doing' versus business skills.

'Doing' or technical skills

Website design	Photography	Knitting	Sewing	Graphic design
Baking	Writing	Painting	Teaching	Editing
Crochet	Screen printing	Jewellery making	Singing	Design

Business and marketing skills

Planning	Budgeting	Negotiating	Selling	Customer service
Trend forecasting	Bookkeeping	Project management	Presenting	Computer skills
Social networking	Digital marketing	Copywriting	Website design	Leadership

Of course, there are some skills that could be classed as both 'doing' and business skills. For example, working as a photographer and using your own photographs on your business website, as photography is both a 'doing' and a business skill. But in many cases, the primary skills needed for actually making your product will be different from the skills you need to manage and grow your business.

Recognize the skills you already have

If you're looking at this list and worrying that you don't have the skills you need to start a business, STOP. Even if you don't have formal training, qualifications or business experience, I bet you've developed quite a few skills throughout your life and career that will come in very handy indeed for your business. What skills have you picked up as a parent, fundraiser, hen party organizer, volunteer, group co-ordinator, student or wedding planner? What are you naturally good at?

To work out what skills you might have, cast your mind right back throughout your life and career, not just the last few years. But if you find identifying your skills tricky, don't worry. Lots of us aren't used to talking about ourselves or thinking about our good points! A definite pattern I've noticed with the creative people (and especially women) I've worked with is that they are great at pointing out the things they are bad at – but generally quite poor at pinpointing the things they are good at!

If you find identifying your skills hard, here are some things to think about that may help you:

- Think back to appraisals or performance reviews in your current or previous day jobs. What have managers, supervisors or mentors praised you for?

- What are people always asking you for help with or to do for them. Organizing parties? Managing the household budget? Planning the annual holiday?

- What 'doing' or technical skills do you have that could become business skills in a different context? For example, if you work in public relations, you could write press releases to promote your new business.

- If you're still stuck, ask friends or family for some pointers. It's often much easier to identify what other people are good at than to do this for yourself!

When I started Handmade Horizons (www.handmadehorizons.com), an online training course for creative business owners, with my business partner Polly Dugdale in 2012, I'd been helping retailers with their online marketing for many years. So I knew how to carry out the hands-on job of selling products and services online. But I had absolutely no idea where to start with developing a membership website or launching a business of my own. So I did the same thing as you've done: I bought a book, got stuck in, and developed the skills I needed as I went along. If I can do it, so can you!

Once you have thought about this, it's time to get started with your next worksheet.

WORKSHEET

For this worksheet, I want you to think carefully about what passions and skills you already have. Remember, you don't need to be an expert at any of these things. You just need to be good enough to handle the basics. If you identify skills you DON'T have, this is good, too! It means you have worked out what areas you might need help with. There are lots of great resources for you to refer to at the end of this book (see Resources), and these aren't skills you need to master overnight.

What are your passions, hobbies and interests? Make a list here:

What skills do you have that could help you in your business? Make a list here:

GET SET FOR SUCCESS

Now you've spent some time thinking about the type of business you want to have, it's time to set yourself up for success! Here are a few things you can do now – BEFORE you get stuck in – that will make working on your business a lot more enjoyable and help you get more done.

Anything you can do to make your workspace more appealing will help to keep you motivated and stay on track!

Find somewhere to work

You don't necessarily need to have a dedicated office or separate room to start a business. Plenty of successful businesses have been started from the kitchen table, after all! But it definitely helps to have somewhere you can a) work without being interrupted and b) keep your things, without having to clear them away every time you want to stop working. The latter is obviously more pressing the more 'stuff' you have: for example, if you're thinking of making products you'll need more space than if you're going to be writing e-books.

Personally I think it's really important to have a space you can retreat to where you get your 'business head' on, especially if you're working from home. Even if it's just a desk in your bedroom or a room where you can work for an hour without disruptions. Of course, if you live alone then you might have the opposite problem – you might be looking for company rather than to escape family members and kids! If this is the case, perhaps you could consider working from a café, library or co-working space a couple of times a week? Take a look online to see what is available in your area.

Get a filing and back up system in place

Although this goes against the grain for lots of creative people (myself included), it really does make sense to get a filing system in place from Day One. As you get ready to launch your business, you'll be writing materials for your website or online shop, keeping notes and maybe even taking photographs, so it makes sense to keep them all in one place.

Online or cloud-based solutions make it really cheap and easy to keep your documents safe and secure too, so there's no risk of losing work if your computer crashes or something else goes amiss. Two solutions that I highly recommend for getting organized online are Google Drive (drive.google.com) and Dropbox (www.dropbox.com); both are free to get started, so why not take a look?

Google Drive

This makes it easy for you to create and update documents online, including spreadsheets and text. You just create, write and save – then your work is all in one place.

Dropbox

This is even more sophisticated because it synchronizes all your personal documents and folders, and stores them in the cloud. This means you can access them from any computer or mobile device, even if you're not online.

Schedule time for your business

Something else I would highly recommend is to schedule time to spend on preparing your business. Before you get started working through each week in this book, have a look through it and think about how much time you'll need to spend reading, completing the worksheets and doing the actual hands-on things recommended each week. Then set aside some time in your calendar so you know exactly when you'll be tackling each area.

If you don't already have a diary or calendar system you use, why not check out Google Calendar (www.google.com/calendar)? Again this service is free to use, will synchronize with your smart phone, and you can even set up reminders to let you know when an appointment (work time!) is about to start.

Here are some other tips to help you get more done while working on your business:

- Avoid distractions. Easier said than done, I know. But try to think ahead. Don't go near Facebook (seriously) during your work times. Put on headphones. Get someone to watch the kids and, whatever you do, don't answer the phone.

- Get into the habit of asking yourself: 'What is the most important thing I need to do today?' This will help you focus and stay on track. Always do the most important task or activity first; you can move onto anything else later if you have time.

- Don't be fooled into thinking that if you don't have a solid block of hours to spend on your business, it's not worth doing. You'll be surprised at how much you can get done in a small amount of time. Even 20 minutes is great!

- If you're feeling downhearted, look back through this book and see how much you have achieved! If you get behind, don't beat yourself up. Just ask yourself what you need to do to get back on track...and make a plan.

- Feeling fed up? Put on some good tunes and have a happy dance. It feels completely stupid sometimes, and like the last thing I want to do. But it works (almost) every time!

CHOOSE YOUR PRODUCT OR SERVICE

So far you've identified your passions, hobbies and interests, as well as some skills that could help you in your business. Now it's time to start thinking about the products and services you could create then sell to turn your passion into profit online. Perhaps you already have a clear idea in mind of the type of product or service you would like to offer? If so, that's great. But if not, here are some options for you to consider:

Sell products

If you have a passion and talent for making or collecting things, why not start an online shop? Whether you love to create original artworks, bake cakes, knit sock monsters or collect vintage papers, there's huge potential to sell your products to people who don't have the skill or time needed to create or search out these products themselves. Hundreds of thousands of artists, designers, makers and other creators have developed a successful business by selling physical products online, and you can do it too!

If you're a maker, you could sell bespoke items made to order, as well as 'off the shelf' products made in advance

Sell digital products

If you love designing, you could sell e-books containing patterns or templates, or pre-made graphics for customers to buy online. Sites like Craftsy (www.craftsy.com) make it easy to sell patterns and tutorials, so you can make money by passing on your expertise. If your passion is food and drink, you could create an e-book containing your most popular recipes for people to cook at home.

A great advantage of digital products is that once you have created them, you can sell them again and again. However, don't be fooled into thinking selling digital products is an easy get-rich-quick scheme. As with any business, areas like marketing, customer service and finance all need to be taken care of, too.

Sell kits

Craft and baking kits have become very popular over the past couple of years, thanks to the explosion of interest in DIY and craft culture. If you've got the knowledge, skills and passion to select the right materials and combine them with instructions or e-books, kits could be a great way for you to make money from your passion online. Kits are also great because they are usually less time-consuming to create than finished physical products. This means they can actually be more profitable for you as a business owner, even if the amount you charge for each item is less.

Sell services

Could any of your passions and skills form the basis of a service offering? Examples of services that customers might be willing to pay for include logo design, product photography and wedding planning – all of these can be sold online, either as a package or by offering your skills at an hourly rate. If you're thinking about selling services, one thing to consider is your geographic location. Is there a need for your particular service in your area, or can you deliver your service online?

Provide teaching and workshops

If you're passionate about your hobby or interest and like helping people, have you considered teaching? Lots of people are very happy to pay somebody to teach them a new skill, or help them improve on an existing one, especially if it means they will get up to speed quickly, . Could you offer one-to-one or group teaching via classes or workshops, offer video tutorials on your website or get paid to offer advice on Google Helpouts (helpouts. google.com)? Perhaps you could even create an e-course, like Polly and I did with Handmade Horizons.

Choose your product or service
WORKSHEET

Use this worksheet to write down as many ideas for products and services as you can think of. Don't censor your ideas at this point, as you'll come back and refine your ideas later on.

CASE STUDY

★ JOLYNE COLBURN ★

Owner of Rowdy Roddy Vintage

Jolyne Colburn is the owner of Rowdy Roddy Vintage (www.rowdyroddyvintage.com), a unique children's boutique. Originally from California, Jolyne now lives in Glasgow, Scotland where she sells a curated collection of vintage and designer clothes for stylish kiddos all over the world from her boutique and online store.

When and why did you decide to start your business?

Being a vintage lover since forever, I started Rowdy Roddy after moving from San Francisco to Glasgow to be with my husband. The business grew from a very big vintage collection that simply became out of control.

Soon after the move our son Roddy was born. I'd started collecting vintage baby clothes while I was pregnant, so I'd ended up with a huge stash. Roddy's dad is in the music business and is away a lot, and I didn't know many people in the UK at that time.

I started selling my collection at vintage and craft fairs with Roddy in tow... And we had such a great time that I decided to find Rowdy Roddy Vintage a permanent home!

You have a bricks and mortar boutique as well as an online shop – which came first?

I opened the shop first then realized I was missing a trick by not selling online. To start off with I chose to sell from Big Cartel (bigcartel.com) because the site was user friendly and the price was right for what I wanted to do.

I would definitely recommend Big Cartel to anyone just starting out. The site is super easy to use and there are templates to suit everyone's needs. And you can't beat the price for a small business, either!

As my business grew, it outgrew Big Cartel. I needed a range of more than 300 products and the site simply doesn't offer that type of plan. So I moved up to a bigger beast, Shopify (www.shopify.com). Now I absolutely love Shopify! Although it's more expensive, my new website looks great.

What have been your proudest moments so far?

Rowdy Roddy Vintage has been featured in the press and in some great blogs... I've even been shortlisted for a Mumpreneur UK award! We have happy customers all over the world, and I love connecting with other ma's and pa's, thanks to the joys of social media sites such as Twitter, Instagram and Facebook.

What advice would you give to someone just starting out?

Take your time, and don't spend money on things you don't need. When I first started out I spent money on things that had zero benefit, like print advertising and employing the wrong kind of staff. That said, it's all a learning experience! Get out there, meet people, and don't be afraid to ask for help.

CHECKLIST

Now you have completed Week One, use this checklist
to see how far you have come!

- [ ] You know what kind of business you want to have, and what you'd like your day-to-day experience of running a business to be like

- [ ] You've created a vision board that represents your dream business

- [ ] You've identified your passions, skills and interests, and have thought about how these could help you in your business

- [ ] You've organized your workspace and set aside time to work on your business each week

- [ ] You've thought about the products and services you could sell, and written a list of initial ideas

WHAT DO
MY CUSTOMERS
WANT?

===== *Week Two* =====

Welcome to Week Two! This week we're going to
be shifting attention from you to another very
important person or indeed group of people:
your CUSTOMERS.

We'll be asking you to start thinking about the
customers you would like to attract, and to create a
dream customer profile that will help you throughout
the rest of this book. We'll also be helping you refine
your list of business ideas and deciding which
product or service you want to sell to them.

It's an action-packed chapter, so let's dive on in!

IDENTIFY YOUR CUSTOMERS

Now you have completed Week One, you'll have a clear idea of:

· Your passions and skills

· Some ideas for products and services you could sell online

· A list of potential products and services you could create yourself

Before deciding which business idea to take forward and deciding on your product or service offering, there's another important question for you to consider:

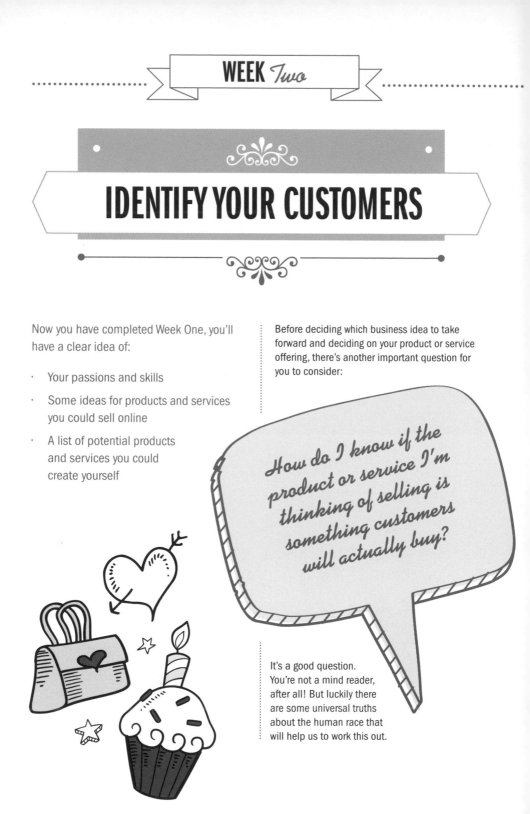

How do I know if the product or service I'm thinking of selling is something customers will actually buy?

It's a good question. You're not a mind reader, after all! But luckily there are some universal truths about the human race that will help us to work this out.

Reasons that people buy

Very broadly speaking (and I am vastly over-simplifying years of psychological research here) whatever the product or service you are offering, people will buy it because of one of three reasons:

- It solves a problem
- It meets a specific need
- It fulfils a desire or dream – for example, of having a particular lifestyle or belonging to a specific peer group

Some examples

- It's Debbie's seven-year-old son's birthday, so she needs to buy him a present. It's not an option. As time goes on, there becomes a pressing need for Debbie to find a gift that her son loves, and one that can be delivered on time.

- Susan is getting married, and dreams of having a unique, bohemian wedding that reflects her personal style. Finding the perfect bespoke wedding stationery is both a question of need (she needs to send out invites so that people will come to her wedding), and of fulfilling a dream.

- Jenny is a PR executive in her early 20s who lives in New York. Finding a one-off dress that's on-trend and that none of her friends will have is fulfilling a dream of living a lifestyle and being esteemed by her peers. It could also be meeting a need, if she needs a dress for a specific event.

As you can see, each different customer has different wants, needs and dreams. These will change over time, and will be different according to the particular product or service in question.

Understand people's wants or needs

Generally speaking, people will go further to solve a problem or meet a need than they will to fulfil a desire or dream. For example, if my computer breaks I NEED to find somebody to fix it, as I must have that problem resolved as quickly as possible. I'm also willing to pay whatever it takes to get the machine back up and running as soon as possible.

Wants or desires are not usually as pressing, though they can become more so with time. For example, I really WANT an Apple MacBook Pro. Apple has done an excellent job of making that product appeal to me. Everything from the branding and advertising to the look of the product and packaging reinforces the fact I want that product. However, it's very expensive, so no matter how much I try to justify the expense I know that although I want it, I don't need it. Therefore I'm willing to delay making a purchase until such time that I have enough spare money lying around. Or that Apple decide to run a promotion that is too good for me to refuse.

However, don't make the mistake of thinking that people won't spend money on products that don't solve a problem or meet a need, or that there isn't a market for luxury items – because there is. Think of high-end fashion and interiors, jewellery and art; you could argue that nobody really needs a diamond necklace, yet thousands are sold for thousands of pounds every year.

We'll delve more into this in the next section. For now though, the key thing to think about is whether there are one or more groups of people who will want or need each of the product or service ideas you noted down at the end of Week One. On your next worksheet, you'll start validating your ideas and work out which one you want to go forward with. Are you excited to get started? I hope so! Let's crack on.

Identify your customers

WORKSHEET

Use this worksheet to identify groups of people who might want or need the product and service ideas you wrote down at the end of Week One. This will help you establish whether there is a market for the product or service you're thinking of offering, and which creative business idea you would like to move forward with.

When you have made your list, read through it. Do any particular ideas jump out? Are there ideas that seem to have more potential than others? Bear in mind that we're not necessarily looking for the idea with the biggest number of potentially interested customers. Niche is often good! But being able to clearly identify a group of potential customers, however small, is great to start off with.

If you think your idea might be too novel or niche there's an easy way to validate your idea. Simply type the name of the product or service you're thinking of offering into your favourite search engine. If there are a few other businesses offering the same product or service, this is a good thing. It means there is an existing market you can tap into. If no one else is offering a similar product or service to the one you're thinking about, generally speaking this isn't a great sign.

I'm not saying that you couldn't build a business by offering a product or service that is completely original and has never been done before. But tapping into an existing market will make it much easier for you to get started and make some sales. So give it some thought, and use this process to refine your ideas. Once you've decided on the product or service you're going to sell, write the name of it here:

....

....

....

Product or service	Who will want or need it?
Knitted Star Wars animals	Star Wars fans (male collectors), people looking for a unique gift for a Star Wars fan
Custom pet portraits	Animal lovers, people looking for an original gift
Hand-printed notebooks with funny literary quotes	Writers, novelists, book fans, people looking for gifts for all of the above

MAKE FRIENDS WITH SELLING

Up until now, the chances are you have been practising your hobbies and indulging your interests for the pursuit of personal pleasure. Whether you've been collecting vintage clothes, crocheting baby hats for friends or making handmade cards, you've been doing it for fun – there's a reason this book is called 'from passion to profit', after all!

You've no doubt had lots of lovely comments from friends, family and others who admire and appreciate your work. Maybe you've been giving this work away for free as gifts, and the reaction has encouraged you to start a business? But to make money from your hobby, you're going to have to make friends with a concept that might be a bit alien to you: selling.

Shift in mindset

When you think of sales and selling, what words and images come to mind? If you're like lots of creative people, the idea of selling is a bit 'bleurgh'. This means it's time for a shift in mindset. Because if you're actually going to turn your hobby into a business, you're going to need to make money. And if you're going to make money, you're going to have to SELL your product or service.

If this thought is paralyzing you with fear now, I've got some good news. Think of the times you have:

- Convinced your kids to eat their greens or get dressed for school.
- Persuaded your friends to go to your favourite restaurant rather than that boring one down the road.
- Suggested a new way of doing things at work, which actually got taken up.

In all of these situations, you've been selling: you've been putting forward the benefits of doing something, and inspiring other people to take action as a result. Even if you're not the kind of person who you'd imagine would make a good sales person (loud, confident and so on) you can most certainly sell. All you really have to do is change your perspective. Rather than thinking about you and the hobby or interest you love, being able to sell requires that you focus on your customer instead.

And it really is as simple as that! I'm not saying that you need to forget about what you want (remember the dream business exercise you did in Week One?; see Imagine Your Dream Business Worksheet) But a successful creative business depends on discovering the SWEET SPOT between what you love to do, the skills you're good at and what customers will pay you for.

Once you start thinking in terms of your customers' wants and needs, selling your products and services will become a breeze!

KNOW YOUR DREAM CUSTOMER

As we've already discussed this week, understanding your customer is quite possibly the most important thing you can do to set yourself up for business success. We've talked a bit about what customers want, you've thought about the customer groups who would be interested in the product or service you'd like to sell, and by now you should have decided what your offering is going to be. Phew! Well done you!

Now it's time to go one step further and drill down into even more detail about your customers. Just as you thought about your dream business in Week One, now we're going to be building up a picture of your dream customer. Why? Because having a clear idea of your dream customer is going to make every aspect of starting your business a lot easier.

Once you have a picture in your head of your dream customer, it's a lot easier to:

· Decide where to sell your product or service online.

· Decide where to promote your business.

· Write sizzling copy for your website or online shop.

Basically, everything becomes a lot easier when you know your dream customer. If you're finding this hard to believe, you're going to have to trust me when I say this has made a massive difference to my own business and to the businesses of the students I have worked with over the past few years.

Who is my dream customer?

Is having a dream customer the same as having a target market?

Yes, and no. If you've attended any business courses or read business books in the past, you might have been asked to describe your target market. And you might have come up with descriptions like this:

· Women who like bags and live in New Zealand

· Stay-at-home mums who travel a lot

· People who like crafts and want to improve their sewing skills

But imagine for a second how many women who live in New Zealand like buying handbags. Erm, quite a few! And isn't there a big difference between the busy mum who needs a practical bag for days out with the kids, and the businesswoman who wants a stylish satchel for carrying her laptop?

The problem with these kinds of target customer statements is that they are too vague to serve any real purpose when you're starting a creative business. They're not going to help you with any of the practical stuff, like working out which product features to highlight, or even how much to charge.

Think back to last week's lesson where we talked about the problems, needs and wants of customers (see Week One: What Creative Business Do I Want?). Even within demographic groups like stay-at-home mums, you'll find hugely different needs and wants. There will be stay-at-home mums

who travel a lot because they have a high-earning husband who whisks them away for regular weekend breaks. There will also be lots of stay-at-home mums who travel a lot because they love camping and going to festivals with their kids.

To appeal to either one of these customer groups, you'll need to do things differently. You could be offering exactly the same product – for example, let's say a handmade travel bag. But the way you price, promote and position your products or services will be very different according to the type of customer you want to attract.

Why not aim to appeal to lots of different customers at the same time?

Great question! But have you ever heard the expression: 'If you're not talking to someone, you're not talking to anyone'? The problem is that if you try to please too many people and adopt a one-size-fits-all approach, you can end up missing the mark and not connecting with anyone at all.

The other problem with trying to appeal to too many people at once is that it can become very confusing and overwhelming. Remember how we said that knowing your dream customer makes things easier? When you're first starting out and trying to take decisions about your business, it really does make it easier to have one customer profile in mind.

As your business grows you might decide to target different customer profiles. You might have different product or service ranges that appeal to different customers and that is absolutely fine. But to start off with, let's keep things as simple and easy as possible. Don't worry about missing out on potential sales. Let's start off with one dream customer then you can always re-visit this as your business grows.

Next steps

Read through the answers you gave to your dream business questions in Week One (see Imagine Your Dream Business Worksheet). Think about the customers you said you'd like to attract, and what they would be saying about you. Now look at the answers you gave in the customer worksheet earlier this week (see Identify Your Customers Worksheet), about customer groups that you think would like your product or service. In the next worksheet, you'll be getting your creative juices flowing and using your imagination to create a dream customer profile. Looking forward to it? Great! Let's get started.

Know your dream customer

WORKSHEET

As you just read, having a clear picture of your dream customer is going to really help as you work through the rest of this book. So now it's time to create your very own dream customer profile. Once you have a clear idea of who your customer is, you can start to imagine:

- Which websites your customer visits
- Which magazines and newspapers your customer reads
- Who your customer listens to for fashion and shopping advice
- How your customer decides which products to buy, or which service providers to use

We know your customers are unique, just like you. But it really will help to keep one specific customer in mind as you work through this book and when working on your business. Get into the habit of asking yourself: 'What would my dream customer think of this?' Then use the answers you give to guide you.

This exercise is going to work your creative juices and get your imagination working overtime. You may think it's a bit silly and feel tempted to skip it. But please don't! Just go with it, and have fun.

1. Think about your ideal customers and list everything that comes to mind. How old are they? Are they male or female? Where do they live? What do they do? Are they married, single, do they have kids? What are their hobbies, passions and interests?

2. What do your ideal customers have in common? Merge as much of the above to form one customer profile. This person will represent your dream customer, so give him or her a name and write it here

3. Describe your customer's life. Where does he or she live, and who with? What does he or she do in any spare time? What magazines, blogs and newspapers does he or she read? What products and services does he or she regularly buy, and why?

4. Imagine your dream customer is about to buy the product or service you're planning to sell. Why is he or she buying it? What problems will it solve? What needs does it meet? What dreams does it fulfil?

MAKE THEM FEEL SOMETHING

It's easy to get hung up on the visual aspects of your business when you first start out – like your logo, and the look and feel of your website. I'm not saying these elements aren't important or that you shouldn't try to get them right. But I firmly believe that if you want to build a successful creative business, you need to think about something much more important than the way your business looks. You need to think about how you want your customers to FEEL.

Best in class

The best companies and organizations, whether they are small independent retailers or large global brands, make you feel something whenever you interact with them. Whether it's a sense of excitement and anticipation when you stand in line at the Apple Store, or the warm, fuzzy feeling you get as you unwrap the latest purchase from your favourite Etsy seller that just arrived in the mail, it's the feeling that keeps you coming back for more. This is what gets you talking about them and telling all your friends. Feelings are what we remember. Without us even realizing it, feelings sink in.

'People will forget what you said, people will forget what you did, but they will never forget how you made them feel.'
– Maya Angelou

A personal example

My favourite hotel chain in the UK is called Premier Inn. It's a budget hotel chain and the rooms are pretty inexpensive. But these hotels always make me feel special and appreciated when I stay in them.

How do they do that? The staff leave a little card on the bed saying I can request a different pillow if the one I have is too hard or too soft. They have another card in the bathroom saying that if I need additional toiletries to give them a ring.

Come to think of it, I have never actually requested a new pillow or run out of shampoo while staying at a Premier Inn. But the fact they have thought of that detail, and that they're prepared to go to that level of effort for little old me, makes me feel special and appreciated.

What's more, this happens every time I stay. The treatment is consistent, and the quality of my experience doesn't vary whenever I stay with them. Premier Inn is fulfilling my dream of living a luxury lifestyle, even though I'm paying less than £100 a night for a room.

And now for you...

It doesn't matter whether you're selling vintage jewellery to budget-conscious students or luxury cushions to interior designers. I'd argue that everyone wants to feel appreciated; everyone wants to feel special in some way. And it's often easier for small independent businesses to make this happen than it is for big, multinational brands or hotel chains to do so.

So before we get into the nitty-gritty of how and where to sell your products or services, ask yourself this. How do you want your dream customer to feel when he or she buys from you? Do you want the husband buying a gift for his wife to feel relieved and reassured? Or excited and inspired? Do you want your female customer to feel like an eco-warrior when she orders one of your upcycled jewellery pieces? Or a super stylish diva?

There are lots of ways you can influence the way your customer feels – everything from the way you introduce your business on your About page, to the way you write about your products and the way you take care of details such as packaging and customer service. These are all opportunities for you to make a connection with your customers and make them feel a certain way.

We'll cover how to do all of these things later in the book. Now though, give this some thought and get ready to move onto your next worksheet.

Make them feel something

WORKSHEET

Use this worksheet to write down some notes on how you want your dream customer to feel when he or she buys from your creative business. This will then help you as you progress through the rest of this book.

1. Think about your favourite blogs, magazines, shops, websites, artists, hotels, restaurants, authors, singers and bands – the ones you would go back to again in a heartbeat. How do they make you feel when you interact with them?

2. What specific things do they do that make you feel this way, however small?

3. Now make a note of what you want your dream customer to feel when they:

· First discover your website or online shop

· Communicate with you by email or on the phone

· Place their first order with you

· Unwrap their order or finish a service they've just bought from you

CASE STUDY

★ KERRY BURKI ★

Editor of
Handmade Success

Kerry Burki is the editor of Handmade Success (www.handmadesuccess.com), a blog and support community for creative business owners. She is also a yoga instructor, a small business advisor and a passionate supporter of the handmade community. Kerry lives in Arizona, USA and helps creative business owners all over the world via Handmade Success and her own website (www.kerryburki.com).

You have successfully combined your passions for yoga, the handmade and helping people through your business. How did you do it?

I just kept saying 'yes' to opportunities that got me excited. Not all of them have worked out, but they have all moved me closer to doing the work I'm currently doing, and I've created some amazing relationships and connections along the way. Honestly, I've helped out for free, bartered and worked for very little money, all in support of businesses I cared about. I believed that these experiences could lead to future testimonials, client work and collaborations – and in my case they all have!

What advice would you give to other multi-passionate people when trying to decide what business to start?

I spent a lot of time thinking about what kind of business to start. As I couldn't quite think of one, it never got started and I kept my interests separate. After moving to Arizona last year I became friends with the owner of a local artisan market. Many of her artists loved the work I was doing on Handmade Success and also said they would benefit from yoga and self-care. So I started my business offering workshops that combine yoga, craft and creative business advice!

I would encourage you to pay attention to connections between your passions then I believe the work you were meant to do will begin to reveal itself. Most of all: stop worrying about what other people will think of you – something that has held me back in the past – and go for it!

It's not always easy being a creative business owner and having to take decisions on your own. What advice would you give to someone who is having doubts or feeling overwhelmed?

Something I do every day is to take at least five minutes of quiet time. This is when answers and ideas come to me and when I get clarity about issues. It also gives me the opportunity to be in the present moment and to accept myself and my current situation as they are. Taking time like this and in a few other ways is a big part of how I help others in business and life.

Is there one piece of advice you wish someone had given you when you were first starting out?

You can get paid to be yourself and to share your interests and knowledge. If you don't happen to know what those are, you'll have to slow down a bit and start to notice where your passion lies, and also what you're knowledgeable about. It might be a whole lot more than you think!

CHECKLIST

You've completed Week Two – well done you! Use this checklist to see how far you have come.

- ☐ You've refined your initial list of ideas and decided what product or service you'll sell

- ☐ You've made friends with sales, and realized that you've been selling all your life

- ☐ You've thought about the problems, wants and needs of your customers

- ☐ You've created a dream customer profile for your business, which will help you throughout the rest of this book and beyond

- ☐ You've identified how you want your customers to feel when they interact with you and your brand

HOW DO I SELL MY PRODUCTS OR SERVICES ONLINE?

=== *Week Three* ===

Welcome to Week Three! This week we're going to be looking at your options for selling your products or services online.

As well as a directory of online marketplaces and my recommendations for e-commerce shop solutions for creative business owners, you'll find some advice on pricing your products and services. Last but not least, you'll be finishing off the week with your one-page business plan, which isn't nearly as scary as it sounds.

Are you eager to get started? Good! Let's go.

CHOOSE YOUR VIRTUAL BUSINESS HOME

Now you've decided which products or services you're going to be selling, it's time to work out where to base your creative business online – aka your virtual business home! Here's a quick overview of your various options:

Use a marketplace shop to sell products

If you're planning to sell products online, the quickest and easiest way to get started is often to open a marketplace shop. Marketplaces like Etsy, eBay and Folksy (see Online Marketplaces Directory) provide you with the opportunity to tap into a ready-made community of buyers, and can prove a cost-effective way to enter the world of selling online.

Most marketplaces charge you a commission when an item sells, and often a small listing fee, too. Some charge a joining fee, and others charge a monthly or annual subscription in return for unlimited listings or extra promotional tools. Some marketplaces allow you to sell downloadable products, such as e-books and patterns, as well as physical goods such as jewellery, fashion and food.

In most cases you'll be responsible for shipping orders and dealing with customer services when you sell items from your marketplace shop. Although the exact process can vary, the marketplace generally takes payment for each order from the customer, then passes it on to you after deducting the agreed commission or fee.

Use a marketplace shop to sell artwork and designs

As well as marketplaces selling physical goods that you create (or source) and sell, a growing number of them provide you with the opportunity to make money from your artwork and designs. Marketplaces like Society6 and Zazzle (see Online Marketplaces Directory) let you offer your designs to potential customers, who can choose to have them printed on t-shirts, gadget covers, stationery and even fabrics.

These marketplaces usually take care of making then posting the goods to customers, and pay a commission or royalty to the artist who created the design. Generally speaking these percentages are pretty small, so you need to put some effort into promoting your designs to generate a meaningful income this way. That being said, you don't have to deal with making, shipping or customer service, which can make this option pretty attractive for some people.

Use your own website to sell products and services

Although creating your own website will usually involve more initial work than starting a marketplace shop, it doesn't have to be difficult! These days there are lots of website solutions specifically designed for designers, makers and creative business owners. Some of these make it easy for even the biggest technophobe to get an e-commerce website up and running in just a few minutes, which means you can sell products and services to customers all over the world. Although there are plenty of free solutions available, you'll probably end up paying a monthly fee if you want to sell your products and services online.

Sell from a blog

If you already have a blog or know you want to start one, adding PayPal buttons to a page on your blog can be a really easy way to start selling a service or even a small number of products. Examples of products and services you could easily offer from your blog include e-books, logo design packages and consultations. If you want to sell workshops or events, take a look at Eventbrite (www.eventbrite.com), an online platform that makes it really easy to sell event tickets to customers from your own website or blog page.

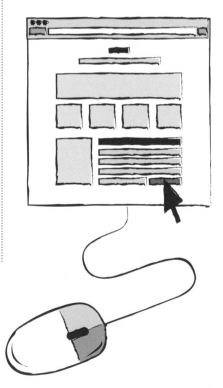

Should I sell from a marketplace shop or my own website?

Remember we are aiming to start your creative business in six weeks or less, so think about the time and resources you have at your disposal over the next few weeks when making your decision on the best option to choose.

Marketplaces

The good bits

- Very quick and easy to get started – no technical skills are required
- Positions your shop and products in front of a ready-made audience of customers
- Low (or no) up-front costs

The bad bits

- Can be less effective for building your own brand
- You'll still need to put effort into promoting your marketplace shop
- In most cases, you'll pay a commission every time something sells – depending on how much you sell, these costs can mount up

Your own website

The good bits

- Start building your brand from Day One
- The time and effort you put into marketing your website benefits you alone
- Take more control over the look and feel

The bad bits

- Depending on the solution you choose, more patience and/or willingness to learn will be required
- Possibility of higher up-front costs
- No established buyer base to tap into, so you'll need to put more effort into marketing and promoting your online shop

FLOW CHART

Now you've read about the pros and cons of selling on marketplace websites versus your own website, do you have an idea which option you would like to choose? Perhaps you're already clear in your mind that you want to take advantage of the ready-made community of shoppers an online marketplace can provide, or maybe you're committed to building your own brand and search engine presence from Day One. However, if not, you'll find the handy flow chart that follows will help make this decision a little easier for you.

Before you look at it, think back to the answers you gave to the worksheets during Week One:

- What skills and interests do you already have? For example, are you already a web design whiz, or a bit of a technophobe?

- How much time do you have? Are you trying to squeeze in an hour or so on your business each day after work, or do you have big chunks of time you can devote to getting your website or shop set up?

- Do you know anyone who could help you, or will you be doing this alone?

When you're ready, take a look at the flow chart. This will help you work out which is the best option for you, before you review our directories of online marketplaces and e-commerce website providers.

Ready to get started? Great! Let's go.

Online marketplaces

DIRECTORY

ART AND DESIGN MARKETPLACES

Marketplace name	Which countries do they cover?	How much will they charge?	What can I sell?
Threadless www.threadless.com	International	Submit your designs for review by the community; if chosen you'll receive a royalty on sales and could even win cash prizes	T-shirts 
Society6 www.society6.com	International	Free to set up; you decide the prices and make a mark-up profit when products sell	Your designs printed as artwork, iPhone covers, clothing, artwork and gifts
Skreened skreened.com	International	Free to set up; you decide the prices and make a mark-up profit when products sell	Your designs printed on adult and kids clothing; t-shirts, hoodies, etc

One of the questions I get asked all the time is: 'Which is the best marketplace for me to sell my products online'? The annoying answer (sorry!) is that there really isn't any such thing as the 'best' online marketplace. The best marketplace for you will depend on lots of factors such as what and where you plan to sell, and the ethos and vibe that appeals to you. Take a look at the following listing of online marketplaces to discover which one might be the best solution for your own products or services.

Best for...	Best bits...	Downsides
Artists, designers	· Fun, attractive website · Massive customer base and social following	· Only chosen designs are made and sold
Artists, designers	· Attractive, mobile friendly website · Easy to use	· Royalties can be small as you only receive a small percentage of the selling price
Designers	· Great seller support · Good quality and ethically sourced merchandise	· As with all design marketplaces, you'll need to promote your designs outside Skreened to become successful

ART AND DESIGN MARKETPLACES continued...

Marketplace name	Which countries do they cover?	How much will they charge?	What can I sell?
Redbubble www.redbubble.com	International	Free to set up; you decide the prices and make a mark-up profit when products sell	Your designs printed on posters, t-shirts, calendars, gadget covers, etc
Spoonflower www.spoonflower.com	USA	10 per cent commission on sales using your design	Your designs printed on fabric, wallpaper, decals and gift wrap
CafePress www.cafepress.co.uk	International	Basic shop is free, Premium shop starts from $6.95 USD per month; you set the price then earn a royalty on sales from your CafePress shop or 10 per cent commission on sales from the Cafepress marketplace	Your designs printed on posters, t-shirts, calendars, gadget covers, etc
Zazzle www.zazzle.co.uk	International	Free to set up; you earn a royalty depending on the product sold, plus a 15 per cent referral fee by signing up to the Zazzle affiliate program	Your designs printed on posters, t-shirts, calendars, gadget covers, etc

Best for...	Best bits...	Downsides
Artists, photographers	· Well-established marketplace · Good quality products	· As with all design marketplaces, you'll need to promote your designs outside Redbubble to become successful
Designers	· Super website · Great community vibe	· To be successful, you'll need to promote your designs outside Spoonflower
Artists, designers	· Great choice of products	· Basic shop is limited with only one design per product type permitted · You'll need to put effort into driving customers to the shop in order to make sales
Artists, designers	· Good community support · Earn a commission by promoting your products and others via the affiliate program	· As with all these marketplaces, you will need to put effort into driving customers to the shop in order to make sales

FASHION AND JEWELLERY MARKETPLACES

Marketplace name	Which countries do they cover?	How much will they charge?	What can I sell?
ASOS Marketplace marketplace.asos.com	International	Business sellers pay £20 per month and a 20 per cent commission when products sell	Fashion and clothing: new, pre-owned and vintage
Scoutmob scoutmob.com	USA	Not strictly speaking a marketplace; pays you a wholesale price for your products in small consignments (10-20 items) then sends you the orders to fulfil	Clothing, jewellery, food, homewares and art
The Wedding Mile theweddingmile.com	USA	6 per cent commission on sales	Handmade and vintage wedding items
Boticca en-gb.boticca.com	International	35 per cent commission on sales	Jewellery and accessories
RebelsMarket www.rebelsmarket.com	International	15 per cent commission on sales	Clothing, jewellery, homeware; anything with an alternative vibe

Best for...	Best bits...	Downsides
Fashion and jewellery designers, collectors	· The only truly international marketplace dedicated to fashion · Sell to fashion-focused customers all around the world · Marketplace boutiques include an integrated blog feature within the price · Mobile friendly website and app	· Fixed cost of £20 per month applies even if you don't make any sales
Indie retailers, designers, makers, local business owners	· Great website · Tap into a massive user base with over 1 million users in the USA	· You need to get your pricing right to be able to sell at wholesale price
Designers, makers	· Great seller support · Very active on social media	· A smaller but growing marketplace
Jewellers	· Attractive, shopper friendly website · European-based but sells worldwide	· Relatively high commission compared to other marketplaces
Designers, makers, artists	· Niche marketplace · Lots of website visitors and big social media following	· Relatively high commission compared to other marketplaces

CRAFT AND GIFT MARKETPLACES

Marketplace name	Which countries do they cover?	How much will they charge?	What can I sell?
ArtFire www.artfire.com	International	$12.95 USD per month subscription	Handmade, vintage, craft supplies, digital products and fine art
eBay www.eBay.com	International	Depends on the category; expect to pay a listing fee per item, plus a variable commission when your item sells	Almost anything! Vintage collectibles, fashion, gifts, craft supplies, food and drink
Etsy www.etsy.com	International	A listing fee on each item, plus a 3.5 per cent transaction commission when your item sells	Handmade, vintage, craft supplies and digital products

Best for...	Best bits...	Downsides
Designers, makers, collectors, craft sellers	· Quick and easy to get up and running · Sell to customers around the world · Good alternative to Etsy if you want a community vibe	· Website feels very US-focused despite being international · Far lower traffic than Etsy
Craft sellers, collectors	· Tap into a massive international customer base · Very easy to get up and running and to sell to customers all over the world · Mobile friendly website and app	· Lots of competition from sellers offering imported or manufactured products at low prices · Shoppers on eBay are more likely to be looking for a bargain than a quality product from a creative business · Selling fees can add up
Designers, makers, artists, craft sellers, collectors	· World's number 1 destination for handmade, vintage and art and craft supplies · Massive engaged customer base · Very easy to get up and running and to sell to customers all around the world · Great community support · Mobile friendly website and app	· With over 1 million sellers worldwide, getting your products seen requires constant effort · Lots of competition means downward pressure on prices

CRAFT AND GIFT MARKETPLACES continued...

Marketplace name	Which countries do they cover?	How much will they charge?	What can I sell?
Craftsy www.craftsy.com	International	No listing fees, no commission	Craft patterns and tutorials
Madeit www.madeit.com.au	Australia	$0.35 AUD listing fee and 4.5 per cent commission on sales	Handmade goods made in Australia
Misi www.misi.co.uk	Europe	£0.20 per listing and 3 per cent commission on sales	Handmade, vintage items and craft supplies
DaWanda en.dawanda.com	International	5 per cent commission on sales; listing fees may apply for multiple categories	'Products with love': handmade, vintage, craft supplies, furniture, art and digital products

Best for...	Best bits...	Downsides
Designers, makers	· With no listing fees or commissions, selling on Craftsy is completely free · Easy to get up and running · Great, shopper friendly website	· Fairly new, so smaller customer base than more established sites like Etsy and Artfire
Craft sellers	· Established marketplace with strong community following · Easy to use	· Only items that have been handmade by you can be sold (no vintage)
Craft sellers	· Low commission · Strong sense of community	· Lots of low value items for sale means it can be difficult to charge higher prices for your work
Designers, makers, artists, craft sellers, collectors	· Truly international: DaWanda have Polish, Italian, French, Spanish, Italian and Dutch websites as well as English language · Ship to anywhere in the world · Mobile friendly website	· All prices are listed in Euros, so the site can be confusing for buyers outside Europe

CRAFT AND GIFT MARKETPLACES continued...

Marketplace name	Which countries do they cover?	How much will they charge?	What can I sell?
Zibbet www.zibbet.com	International	Free for up to 50 listings per month, then $9.95 USD per month for a premium subscription	Handmade, vintage, craft supplies, digital products and art
Felt felt.co.nz	New Zealand	$0.50 NZD listing fee per item plus 5 per cent commission on sales; additional $0.30 NZD to list products in an extra category	Handmade goods
Yumbles www.yumbles.com	UK	18 per cent commission plus £0.30 flat fee on sales	Food and drink, including gifts
Folksy folksy.com	UK	Basic account = £0.15 plus VAT per listing, plus 6 per cent commission; Plus account = £45 p/a (unlimited listings) plus 6 per cent commission	Handmade items and craft supplies
Not on the High Street www.notonthehighstreet. com	UK	£199 joining fee plus 25 per cent commision on sales	Unique handmade items and gifts

Best for...	Best bits...	Downsides
Designers, makers, artists, craft sellers, collectors	· Free for up to 50 listings per month	· Much smaller than Etsy with a smaller (but growing) customer base
Designers, makers, jewellers, craft sellers	· Attractive layout · Easy to use	· Open to all handmade sellers so plenty of competition
Indie retailers	· Attractive website · Great seller support	· Membership on an application basis
Handmade British crafts	· Great support and community vibe · Dedicated to British craft	· No vintage items
British gifts and crafts	· Lots of advertising and promotion = lots of sales for successful sellers	· Relatively expensive and membership is on an application basis

E-commerce websites
DIRECTORY

Website name	How much will they charge?
Shopify www.shopify.com	From $29 USD per month (plus 2% transaction fee) up to $179 USD per month
Storeenvy www.storenvy.com	Free, but $5 USD per month if you want a custom domain (recommended)
Squarespace www.squarespace.com	From $8 USD for one product up to $24 USD for unlimited products per month with no start-up or transaction fee
SupaDupa supadupa.me	From £0 for 10 products up to £49 for unlimited products per month

If you've decided you're going to take the plunge and sell your products or services from your own website rather than listing them on an online marketplace, your next big decision is which website solution to choose. Here I've created a list of my top ten website providers for creative business owners who want to sell online. These are all companies who provide 'hosted' e-commerce website solutions, which essentially means those designed with non-technical folk in mind! By using one of these solutions, you'll be able to take payments online, update your website from anywhere with an Internet connection, and you won't need to worry about details like purchasing hosting for your website or installing software.

Cool features...	Downsides...	Is there a free trial?
· Fantastic choice of professional looking themes · Easy to use with great help and support · All packages have unlimited products · Great choice if you want a professional shop with lots of features	· Fees can quickly add up if you're selling a lot of items	Yes, 14 days
· Very simple and easy to use – a great starter website · List your products in the Storenvy marketplace · Strong online community	· No integrated blog or mailing list, so adding your own mailing list will require some manual effort · Limited features (yet simplicity is part of the appeal) · Maximum of 500 products	Starter package is free
· Lots of advanced features and tools · Good range of sleek, mobile friendly designs · Integrated mailing list and blog	· Features may be overwhelming for the beginner	Yes, 30 days
· Slick, design-focused templates ideal for creative businesses	· No integrated blog or mailing list	Starter package is free

Website name	How much will they charge?
IndieMade www.indiemade.com	From $4.95 USD for 10 products up to $19.95 USD for up to 300 products per month with no start-up or transaction fee
Big Cartel bigcartel.com	From $9.99 USD for 25 products up to $29.99 USD for 300 products per month with no start-up or transaction fee
Create www.create.net	From £5 for 100 products to £36 for 10,000 products per month with no transaction fee
Volusion www.volusion.co.uk	From £9 for 100 products to £89 for unlimited products per month with no transaction fee
Madefreshly madefreshly.com	From $0 USD for 10 products (no custom domain and only one product image) to $34.99 USD (500 products) per month
Bigcommerce www.bigcommerce.com	From $24.95 USD for 100 products to $299.95 USD for unlimited products and bandwidth per month

Cool features...	Downsides...	Is there a free trial?
· Etsy connect feature to push products to Etsy with a single click · Simple to use and get started · Designed for artists and independent business owners	· Maximum 300 products	Yes, 30 days
· Very simple to use and get started · Low cost · Products will be included in the Big Cartel Directory	· Maximum 300 products · Fairly limited in terms of themes and designs	Starter package is free
· Good support via account manager and community forum	· UK-based support could be a negative for customers in other countries · Not as easy to use as some of the other solutions	Yes, 30 days
· More cost-effective solution for larger shops with more products · Lots of tools and features · Sell your products on eBay and Amazon	· Cheaper plans have lower bandwidth and high costs if you exceed your limits · More complicated to use than some of the other solutions · Cost of added features can add up	Yes, 14 days
· Easy to use and get started	· Very limited features in the free account	Starter package is free
· Lots of advanced features and tools · Offers an unlimited bandwidth package	· Fairly limited choice of themes · You could end up paying for features you don't use	Yes, 15 days

WEEK *Three*

SELECT THE RIGHT ONLINE MARKETPLACE

If you've decided that selling your products or services from an online marketplace is the best option for you, here are three questions you should ask yourself when deciding which one to choose:

1 Would my dream customer shop from this marketplace?

Think back to the dream customer profile you created last week. Can you imagine your dream customer shopping on this website? Some marketplaces are very strong in a particular product category – for example, jewellery or children's clothes – and not so strong in others. Some marketplaces might attract more upmarket customers looking for high value items, while others attract bargain hunters on the look out for a deal. Think about the look and feel of each website and its overall ethos, as well as the types of products and sellers who are already here. If you can't imagine your dream customer shopping on this website, it's unlikely to be the best choice for you.

2 How much will this marketplace cost me?

Does the marketplace charge a joining fee or membership fee? How much commission does it take on sales? Will you be charged every time you list a new product, or only when something sells? Fees aren't necessarily bad: after all, marketplaces are businesses that need to make their money from somewhere, and their big advantage is that they have bigger budgets for marketing and advertising than any individual seller would have on their own. So don't discount marketplaces solely because they charge more money than others, but do your research and make sure you factor in the fees when deciding on how much to charge for the products in your shop.

3 What are other sellers saying about this marketplace?

If you want to find out what creative business owners think about a marketplace, reach out to other sellers on social media and look at community forums. Ask for feedback on things like how easy the platform is to use, and how they'd rate the seller support. However, bear in mind there will always be people who like to complain that they haven't made any sales, and this might not always be the fault of the marketplace.

SELECT THE RIGHT E-COMMERCE WEBSITE

If you've decided you want to run your own e-commerce website, here are three questions for you to ask yourself when deciding which solution to choose:

1 How easy is the website to update and use?

This is really key. If you find updating your website is time-consuming and confusing, you'll soon become frustrated, waste time and end up not doing it as often as you should. So it's worth spending some time finding a platform you're comfortable with. All the online shop providers listed in the directory offer a free package or free trial, so have a play around and take the opportunity to try before you buy.

2 How much will the website cost if my needs change?

Some e-commerce website providers offer a free plan, which can be a great way to start off if you have a small number of products. Free solutions typically provide you with a limited number of free templates to use, and place restrictions in terms of the number of products and pages you can add. If you're happy to sacrifice control for cost in the beginning while you get yourself started, free solutions can be great to get you off the ground.

However you might soon start to find that the free package is too restrictive, and decide you need to move to a paid plan. Always review your options with this in mind – just because a platform offers a free plan, it doesn't mean that this will be your most cost-effective option as your business grows. Try to think ahead and anticipate how your needs might change, as it's a pain to change your website once you're up and running.

3 Which website tools and features do I really need?

Some website solutions have a huge list of added features and marketing tools, which can make them seem better value than others. However, it's important to think about how many of these you'll really need. Added features can bump up the cost, and are only worth the money if you end up actually using them. So before you start thinking about which shop solution to use, make a list of the features and tools you'll really want and need. If you're planning to sell products online, a mobile friendly design, multiple product images, integrated mailing list and analytics program should definitely be on your list.

WHAT ABOUT WORDPRESS?

You'll notice that I haven't included Wordpress.org (wordpress.org) in my list of top ten e-commerce websites. Is that because I don't think Wordpress is a good website platform for selling your products online? On the contrary: I think Wordpress is fantastic, and I regularly use Wordpress myself for my own and for my clients' websites. However, if you want to sell products online and get your website up and running as quickly as possible, Wordpress is not your best option, UNLESS:

- You have used Wordpress.org before, or are familiar with websites and comfortable with things like setting up a hosting account and configuring a domain.

- You have plenty of time and enthusiasm to get stuck in and learn, or can afford to pay somebody else to set up your website for you.

Working with Wordpress.org

The big advantage of Wordpress.org is that it's very flexible and customizable so you can get it to look the way you want; it's also very easy to use once you have it set up. Using Wordpress.org for your online shop can also be a cost-effective solution compared to hosted e-commerce solutions that charge ongoing monthly fees.

However, you'll need to learn how to do things, such as install plug-ins (additional features), make back ups and configure your domain. Of course, I'm not saying you won't be able to do these things – you'll have your own view of how technical you are (or want to be)!

If you do decide to use Wordpress.org to set up an online shop, or you just want to find out more about how this platform works, my recommendation would be to go and have a look at Woo Commerce (www.woothemes.com/woocommerce/). This is a Wordpress plug-in that will turn any self-hosted Wordpress.org website into an e-commerce store. The team at Woo Commerce offer a number of free e-commerce themes, as well as a huge range of plug-ins to manage things like international shipping, product customization and so on.

If you decide you want to use Wordpress.org and would like to find someone to help you get set up, look for recommendations in the blogs in the resources section (see Resources). Many of these blogs will contain marketplaces where creative business advisors and website designers advertise their business support services. As always, it's a good idea to ask for recommendations before you commit to working with someone, so reach out to the online community.

Wordpress.org versus Wordpress.com – what's the difference?

You may have noticed that there are two Wordpress sites – Wordpress.org AND Wordpress.com – and there's a marked difference between the two. Wordpress.com is great for blogging; it's cheap, very easy to use, and comes with lots of great features like spam protection built in. However, Wordpress.com is not good for selling online; there's no e-commerce functionality built in, and options for customization are limited.

Wordpress.org – sometimes referred to as a 'self-hosted' solution, as you are responsible for purchasing hosting for any website you build using its software – is great for building a highly customized, professional website. Wordpress.org is infinitely flexible with thousands of plug-ins and extensions available, such as e-commerce ones for selling products and services online.

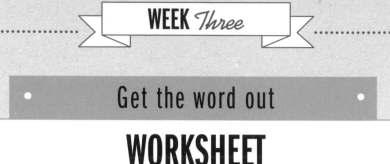

Get the word out

WORKSHEET

Now you've decided where you're going to have your online shop, the next step is to work out how you're going to let people know about it. Sadly, many newbie business owners make the mistake of thinking that they can launch a marketplace or website shop, then relax and wait for the orders to come rolling in. For your business to be a success you need to do more than that – you need to get the word out!

That means proactively promoting your business, and encouraging people to visit your website or online shop. This is also known as...marketing (!), and you can use this worksheet to create your first marketing plan. But before doing this, think again about the dream customer profile you created last week (see Know Your Dream Customer Worksheet). How does that customer decide where to shop? What websites and blogs does he or she visit? What magazines does he or she read?

It's important to keep in mind your own personal resources too, as well as the budget you have available. If you only plan to work on your creative business part-time, it's unlikely you'll be able to manage three social media channels as well as everything else you need to do to keep things running smoothly. Likewise if you have a limited budget, it's unlikely that press advertising (which is expensive) will feature in your early marketing plans.

Rather than spreading yourself too thinly, choose the activity you think will have the biggest chance of reaching and capturing your dream customer's attention. So fill out this worksheet and decide how you'll get the word out.

Where can I find my dream customers?	How can I get my product or service in front of them?	What will I need to do to get started with this?
Pinterest	Create a Pinterest account and pin products from my online shop	Look for information on how to use Pinterest for business, and make sure I have pin-worthy images on my website
Lifestyle blogs	Get in touch with blogs that my dream customer might read, and ask them to write about my work	Create a list of blogs then find out the names of bloggers I should get in touch with
Facebook	Create a Facebook page and let all my friends and family know about it	Learn how to create a Facebook page for my business

WORKSHEET

PRICE YOUR PRODUCTS

Pricing can be a tricky issue that raises lots of 'icky' feelings. But it doesn't have to be! To get you in the right frame of mind to start thinking about this topic, think back to the answers you came up with in Week One (see Imagine Your Dream Business Worksheet)

- What type of customers do you want to be selling to?

- How much do you want to be selling your products and services for?

- How much money do you want to be bringing in?

- How many orders a month do you want to ship?

Price versus profit

Let's say you sell handmade bags, and want to sell them to busy mums who want something handy to throw over their shoulder for the school run. You want to sell them for around £25 each, and have the time and energy to make and ship three bags every week.

Think for a second about that retail price of £25, and imagine you're making a profit of £10 a bag after all your overheads and costs have been taken into account. Multiply that by three bags a week for four weeks in a month, and that gives you a total monthly profit of £120. How does that compare with the amount of money you said you'd like to be making back in Week One?

If it's a lot less, you're going to need to charge more to have any hope of making your target income. Yes, there are other things you could do to increase your profit, such as reducing costs and minimizing overheads. But the likelihood is that the price you were thinking of charging your customers is far too low, and you'll need to get your head around the concept of charging more.

Common pricing mistakes

If you're already thinking 'But nobody will pay more for the product or service I'm going to sell' then STOP. This is a very common trap that creative business owners fall into. The fact is that most people start their business without a clear idea of their overheads and costs. They price towards the bottom of the market, because they think this is what it will take to get customers to notice and to buy from them. Yet often, the opposite is true.

Not charging enough for your product or service can turn customers off, and put them off buying from you. Low prices can leave potential customers wondering about the quality or authenticity of what you have to offer; if you're offering a service, low prices can attract a less-than-desirable customer, too.

What sort of customer would you rather deal with? The customer looking for a bargain, who questions and quibbles over every aspect of the service you provide? Or the customer who is willing to pay for quality, and respects the knowledge and experience you have?

Another common mistake you should avoid making is to base your prices on what you would be willing to pay for a similar product or service yourself. Just because you wouldn't be willing to pay £50 for a necklace, doesn't mean your target customer wouldn't either.

If you're feeling nervous about pricing your products and charging your worth, think about the following points:

- The amount of VALUE you're giving customers with the product or service you have to offer, in terms of the wants and needs it meets, or the transformation it helps your customers achieve.

- The amount of TIME, EFFORT and ENERGY that has gone into creating your product or service, including all the years of hard work that have gone into developing your expertise and craft.

- The UNIQUENESS of your product or service, especially if you're making things by hand.

So how much should I charge?

In the end, how much you charge for your products or services is up to you. It's easy to get too caught up worrying about this at the beginning, and to spend time looking at competitors to see what they charge. This can lead down a slippery slope, so try not to make this mistake. Simply start by getting a rough idea of your overheads and costs, then find a pricing strategy that fits with the products or services you're planning to sell.

Remember!

- How and where you promote your products will have a big impact on how much customers are willing to pay.

- There are lots of ways to increase the perceived value of what you have to offer, from copywriting to photography, that we'll be covering over the next couple of weeks.

- Don't worry if you don't get your pricing right from Day One! You can tweak it and adjust as you find out what works.

Your one-page business plan

WORKSHEET

Now we're almost halfway through this book, take a few minutes to think about how far you've come. You've learned a lot, made lots of key decisions and taken lots of positive action to put the foundations of your business in place! Now it's time to wrap up everything you've done so far, and consolidate your plans into a one-page business plan by filling out your answers to the questions listed here. This isn't nearly as scary as it sounds, but will really help you to focus your ideas before we get into Week Four.

Describing your business

What product or service will you sell?

Who is your dream customer?

What needs or wants will you meet?

Moving from passion to profit

How much will you charge?

How will customers pay you?

Getting the word out

How will you promote your creative business?

How will you help people find out about your business?

Achieving your goals

Within six months of starting my business, I'd like to achieve the following:

Resources required

To achieve the above, I'll need the following resources:

Time:

Money:

Training:

Other:

I'll launch my business no later than (date):

....

WORKSHEET

CASE STUDY

★ ANNIE MCGEE ★

Owner of
Scavenger Annie

Scavenger Annie is an alternative embroiderer and seamstress, who has turned her passion for embroidery into a rocking business. She sells her quirky products from her website (www.scavengerannie.co.uk), as well as sharing her knowledge and passion through her sewing workshops.

How and when did you decide to start your business?

I started my alternative embroidery business three years ago when I was looking for unique clothes for my newly born son. I found that the clothes already out there were just not alternative or 'rocky' enough for my little fella. I came upon the fantastic world of machine embroidery and discovered that this was a great way to customize clothes. My range of quirky threads stitched with a twist now includes everything from customized baby clothes to handmade adult clothing and textiles.

When did you start to sell online?

After a few months of promoting my wares on Facebook, I decided to take the plunge and build my own website and start an Etsy shop, opening both stores at the same time. I found that starting my own business was a huge learning curve, from researching search engine optimization, product photography, website design and building, to gaining knowledge about the administration side of the business. I do feel like a Jack-of-all-trades at times, but that's been the fun part of working for myself – you can never get bored!

What has been your biggest challenge so far?

My biggest challenge has been balancing work, family time and my creative business. When I first delved into the rockin' threads I was working at the day job, looking after my little man and sewing in the evenings. Since being made redundant last year I now have that extra headspace to focus on my business more.

And your proudest moments?

My proudest moments have to be experiencing the support from my friends, family and customers. I recently won a business funding competition and the support I received from everyone sharing, voting and promoting Scavenger Annie was overwhelming. I can't wait to take my business to the next level and share with everyone the latest stitchery and plans for the business.

What would your advice be to anyone else who is thinking of starting a creative business?

I'd have to say, make sure you're clear on what you want to get out of your business. Start off with a business plan (like you're doing in this book!) and always revisit and edit it along the way as your business grows. It will help you stay focused. The opportunities to network with other creatives in the same boat as you are now vast, so do get away from the computer screen once in a while! Meeting people face to face can lead to new information, new contacts and business inspiration.

CHECKLIST

You've completed Week Three – well done you! That's brilliant! Now use this checklist to review everything you've done this week:

- [ ] You've thought about your options for selling online and decided which marketplace or website solution to use (woo-hoo!)

- [ ] You've thought about pricing and how much to charge for your products and services

- [ ] You've thought about marketing and how you'll get the word out

- [ ] You've wrapped up everything you have done so far by creating a one-page business plan

You're amazing!

GETTING DOWN TO BUSINESS

Week Four

Welcome to Week Four. This week we're going to be focusing on the practical elements of getting your website or marketplace shop ready to share with the world.

To help you keep on track, you'll find a handy checklist showing everything you'll need to cover between now and the launch. You'll also find information on the grown-up bits you need to think about, plus fun photography tips.

So take a look at these resources, then get started with creating your online shop or website. Let's get ready to rumble...!

WEEK *Four*

Countdown to launch
WORKSHEET

Tick off each of the following items as you complete them and add them to your online shop over Weeks Four, Five and Six. We'll be covering many of these between now and the end of this book, plus you'll find more information and advice about anything you need more help with in the resources section (see Resources).

Grown-up bits
- [ ] Decide on a business structure
- [ ] Register your business with relevant authorities
- [ ] Purchase insurance (optional)

Branding
- [ ] Business name
- [ ] Logo (optional)
- [ ] About page

Products and services
- [ ] Create and upload images
- [ ] Write product or service descriptions
- [ ] Research and decide on shipping rates
- [ ] Source packaging (optional)

Accepting payments
- [ ] Set up business bank account (optional)
- [ ] Set up PayPal account
- [ ] Test purchase process

Other shop policy pages
- [ ] Contact information
- [ ] Returns and cancellations policy or guarantee
- [ ] Terms and conditions
- [ ] Privacy policy (optional)
- [ ] Delivery information
- [ ] Payment information

Optional extras
- [ ] Register a domain name for your website
- [ ] Set up a business email address
- [ ] Open a Mail Chimp account
- [ ] Set up social media accounts
- [ ] Link your blog to your online shop
- [ ] Add a Frequently Asked Questions page

If there is anything else you need to get ready in order to launch your website or online shop, write it in this space here:

....
....
....
....
....

TACKLE THE GROWN-UP STUFF!

This is where lots of people get stuck and spend ages fretting instead of getting on with things. But you're not going to make that mistake; you're far too savvy for that!

Choose a legal structure for your business

Before you start trading, you'll need to decide on the structure you want to have for your business. There will be different options depending on which country or state you live in, whether you'll be working on your own or in a partnership, and what you plan to do with the profits you make.

Most people who want to start a business by making money from a hobby decide to register as a SOLE PROPRIETOR or SOLE TRADER. The upside of this option is that it's very quick and easy to get started, with minimal paperwork. As a Sole Proprietor or Sole Trader, you'll need to declare your earnings for tax purposes each year, and pay any tax that is due.

Making sure that your business gets off on the right footing is important, but the process doesn't need to be scary.

One downside of being a Sole Trader is that there is no legal differentiation between you and your business, so you're responsible for any costs or debts that your business incurs. Therefore, if you decide that you want more separation between yourself and your business, you might want to consider registering yourself as a LIMITED COMPANY (Ltd) in the UK, a LIMITED LIABILITY CORPORATION (LLC) in the USA, or a PROPRIETARY LIMITED COMPANY (PTY Ltd) in Australia. This will mean additional reporting responsibilities and more paperwork, both of which will probably require the help of an accountant and maybe also a lawyer.

If you don't already have a clear idea of which kind of business structure would be best for you, take a look at the resources for your country (see Resources), and move forwards from there. This doesn't need to be time-consuming or complicated, and there are many sources of free information and advice available online.

Frequently asked questions

At this point your head is probably spinning with questions, or you're tempted to hide under a rock! You're most definitely not alone if you find the legal side of things confusing – and possibly a little bit intimidating. To help you out, here are some of the most frequently asked questions I get asked by soon-to-be creative business owners who are plotting their very first steps. You'll find website addresses for all the organizations mentioned here in the resources section (see Resources).

Who do I need to tell that I have started a business?

Again, this will depend on the country and state you live in, and the business structure you have chosen:

- If you live in the UK and have decided to register as a Sole Trader, you'll need to contact HMRC to advise them within three months of starting your business. You can do this by phone, which is actually far less scary than you might think! When you register as a Sole Trader you'll need to start paying Class 2 National Insurance contributions, but will be able to claim an exemption if you think your earnings will be under around £5,500 per year. HMRC will then register you for self-assessment, which means you'll need to submit a tax return once a year. Find details and the number to call on the HMRC website (see Resources).

- If you live in the UK and have decided to form a Limited Company or alternative legal structure, such as a Partnership or Community Interest Company, in many cases it will be easier to find an accountant or advisor to help you take care of the necessary paperwork. Lots of accountants will offer a free consultation before you start working with them, so you can use this opportunity to get some advice and see if they are a good fit for your business. To find an accountant, ask for recommendations or look online; again, reaching out to the creative community online is a great way to get help and advice.

- If you live in the USA and have decided to register as a Sole Proprietor, you'll need to register your Doing Business As Name (business name) with your City Clerk's Office or your State Government, depending on where you live; if your city requires all businesses to have a business license, you'll need to obtain one from your City Clerk's Office. If you're thinking of starting a Limited Liability Corporation, the exact registration rules vary by state. Whichever option you choose, your first port of call should be to visit the Small Business Association website (see Resources) to find details of your local office then contact them for advice.

- If you live in Australia, you'll need to apply for an Australian Business Number (ABN) by visiting the Australian Business Register website (see Resources). If you're thinking of starting a Proprietary Limited Company, visit the Australian Taxation Office website for up-to-date advice.

For other countries, please refer to the resources section (see Resources) for more details.

Do I need a business bank account?

If you're serious about starting a business, it's a good idea to start a separate business bank account. This makes it much easier to keep track of your income and the money you spend on your business, especially as your business grows. Many banks offer a period of free banking for start-ups, so do some research and see what offers are available.

Do I need a licence to trade?

This depends on what you're planning to sell, and where you live. If you're planning to sell toys or any products aimed at children, skincare, food or drink, it's likely there will be regulations with which you'll need to comply when selling your products online. You may also require a licence if you'll be trading from home with people visiting your workshop. A quick Google search should usually be enough to tell you if you need to investigate further, but do get in touch with your local business advice service or reach out to other creative business owners online if you need specific advice.

Do I need business insurance?

As you won't be employing people at this stage and your business will be conducted online, you shouldn't need Employers Liability or Public Liability Insurance. But depending on what you're planning to sell and the stock you plan to hold, you might want to take out business insurance to cover your costs in case of a fire or loss of equipment, or in case of a claim against your business. The best way to find a suitable business insurance is by making a quick online search, or reaching out to ask other creative business owners which companies they would recommend.

OVERCOME COMMON FEARS

We're now halfway through Week Four, and the launch of your business is in sight. Hopefully you're feeling excited, motivated and eager to bring your business to life. But it's perfectly normal if you're not.

At this point in your journey from passion to profit it's quite common for a few doubts to start creeping in!

- Perhaps you're feeling as though there's too much left to do, and you'll never get it all finished in time?

- Maybe you're starting to wonder if you really want to start a business after all?

- Perhaps you feel like you haven't got the skills or experience that running a business takes, or that your products aren't good enough?

If this is the case then STOP and take a deep breath. Know that these feelings and doubts are perfectly common and natural, but none of them are true.

Understand resistance

These feelings are known as RESISTANCE, a sinister force that lurks within you and threatens to scupper your plans. This force doesn't like change; it wants things to stay the same. Resistance stops countless would-be entrepreneurs in their tracks, and we don't want this to happen to you.

Whether your goal is to eventually quit your day job or to just make some money from your hobby, starting a business involves a massive personal change. You're en route to becoming a business owner and an entrepreneur, and you're about to put your work out into the world! It's perfectly natural to feel scared or nervous.

Being a creative business owner means continually being judged; asking people to say 'yes, I'll buy it', or 'no, I won't'. And just as it's perfectly natural to feel nervous about offering yourself up for judgement, it's entirely natural to want to avoid this altogether. To find a reason to delay launching your business. To wait until you've found the perfect business name, the perfect logo, written the perfect About page, or found the perfect packaging for your perfect products. But DON'T.

Overcome resistance

There will never be the perfect time, the perfect product or the perfect offer. There will always be a better logo, a better shop banner, a more catchy product name or a more compelling description. All the market research in the world won't be able to tell you for sure whether your product or service will be a hit or not. Regardless of how many similar offerings there are out there in the marketplace, there is only one of you.

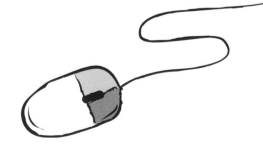

The only way to find out for sure if anyone will buy what you have to offer is to try it out!

Launch your website, open your shop, put your work out there, see what works. There's no denying that this is scary, but your confidence will grow. To make things easier, look for support from people who are either in the same boat as you now, or have been in the same situation as you in the past. Connect with other business owners in your area or online by looking at the resources section (see Resources) to find creative communities you can tap into.

Resistance is natural, but resistance can be overcome. I know you can do it. We're soon going to enter the last two weeks of our journey, and most of your hard work is done. So let's go strong, go hard and get your business launched. You're going to have lots of fun!

GIVE YOUR BUSINESS AN IDENTITY

How do you want the outside world to view YOUR business? Giving your business an identity is an exciting step! This week, you should:

Choose a name for your business

Choosing a business name is an important (and exciting!) step. You might already have a name in mind, which is great. However, before deciding, here are a few important things to think about:

- What image do you want to portray of your business to potential customers? To help you answer this question, think about the answers you gave in the dream business worksheet in Week One (see Imagine Your Dream Business Worksheet).

- Is the domain (website) name that matches that business name available?

- Does your chosen name have any hidden connotations or use in slang that you might not have thought about? Again, a Google search is a good tool to help you research this.

- Will you be able to use the business name to register accounts through social media?

- Has anybody else registered a trademark using this name? To check this out, take a look at the resources section at the end of the book (see Resources).

Create a logo for your business

You'll almost certainly want a logo or banner image for your website or marketplace shop. So if you're not a designer yourself, here are three ways to source a great logo for your creative business:

- Look for creative community recommendations online (see Resources), then hire a designer.

- Purchase a one-of-a-kind logo or banner design on Etsy or another marketplace.

- Create your own logo using the SquareSpace logo tool (www.squarespace.com/logo), which is free for SquareSpace website customers, or $10 USD for anyone else.

PHOTOGRAPH YOUR PRODUCTS

If you're going to be selling products, this week you should be photographing your items and getting them ready to add to your online shop. This should be fun, fun, fun!

Having good quality photographs is probably the most important thing to get right when selling online. Not only will good quality photos help you to stand out from the crowd, but they'll also help you to sell more products and build your brand. Here are three reasons why it's worth spending some time and effort on your photography:

1. When buying online, customers don't have the luxury of picking up and examining your items as they would in a shop. Photographs are one way to overcome this barrier and to give them the confidence they need to buy.

2. Great photos will increase your chances of getting your work featured in blogs and magazines. When was the last time you saw a blurred or dull-looking photograph in a glossy magazine? Exactly! Having a good selection of lifestyle shots – for example, photographs of your items in real life settings – can capture the attention of bloggers and journalists, as well as potential customers.

3. Photography is really key if you're planning on selling on a marketplace shop, too. The lucky people who curate the home pages of websites like Etsy and Folksy pick out the products with the very best photographs, so if you aspire to appearing on the home page of Etsy or other covetable marketplace slots, you need to put some effort into producing drool-worthy shots!

Hopefully by now you're convinced of the need to have great product images to market your creative business. But if you're starting to worry that you don't have the right equipment or can't afford professional help, fear not. These days, it's easier than ever to take good photos. You don't need a fancy camera or expensive equipment right from the start: a smart phone or a compact camera is perfectly adequate.

So it you've already got a fancy camera then great, but if not, don't panic – help is at hand! For this week's Case Study, I asked creative product and lifestyle photographer Holly Booth to share some of her top photography tips with us. To learn more, read on.

CASE STUDY

★ HOLLY BOOTH ★

Creative & lifestyle photographer

Holly Booth has worked with countless creative business owners since starting her photography business back in 2010. Pop over to Holly's website (www.hollybooth.com) to see some examples of her work then read on for her top tips.

What's the best way to start taking photos for my online shop?

As keen as you might be to start snapping away, it's a good idea to spend a few minutes thinking about what photos you're actually going to need for your online shop. As well as the style of the shots – for example, different angles, close-ups, white backgrounds, lifestyle shots – think about the look and feel you want to achieve. Do you want an urban, edgy look, or would a laid-back, country vibe be better for your products?

To help decide this, lots of my clients like to create a mood board by tearing out pictures from magazines; I'm a massive fan of Pinterest, too! Have a look around for inspiration before you get started, and see what look and style appeals to you and would work best for your business.

Also, think about where you'll photograph your work: it's a good idea to shoot somewhere with natural light, so doing this near a big window will generally work well. And gather together any props and equipment you need before you get started; this will make your life much easier and save a lot of stress.

How many photos do I need to take?

Lots! To start off with, you'll need to take plenty of photos and see which ones come out best. Just play around and have fun! Remember, when you're selling online you'll need some close-ups to show the detail of items, as well as photographs of your products positioned alongside props to provide customers with an idea of their size and scale.

How should I style my photographs?

My advice is to keep it simple. Select a few props that you think will work well, then play around with textures in your shots to see what works. While you're doing this, keep your brand and the image you want to portray in your mind at all times.

As well as lifestyle shots, it's useful to take some photographs with white backgrounds, because this is what journalists ask for if they decide to feature your products in a magazine. You don't want to be scrabbling around trying to take photos in a hurry if a journalist does get in touch, so it's definitely a good idea to take a few of these now.

Photographing good product images with white backgrounds doesn't need to be complicated. Set up your shots with sheets of white paper for your background, then use sheets of foam board or white card to reflect light back onto your products when needed. Shoot in natural light or consider buying a light tent from Amazon or eBay – they're not too expensive and they're a good investment, as they're sure to get used as your business grows.

Do I need a fancy camera or DSLR?

Not at all! If you're lucky enough to have a good camera, my top tip would be to read the manual and master the basics first. But if all you have is your smart phone, that's fine too. There are loads of great apps you can use to edit, re-size and even share your images directly from your smart phone, and I've listed some of my favourite photography apps for phones here:

- · VSCOcam
- · Afterlight
- · ProCamera
- · ABeautifulMess

Do I need to buy new software for editing photos?

You don't need to spend a lot of money on expensive software when you're first starting out, as there are lots of free and inexpensive tools you can use to add effects, re-size and add text to photos, and so on. Here are some suggestions for some online photo editing software and tools to try out, so have a play and have fun!

- · GIMP
- · Pixlr
- · iPiccy
- · Photoshop Express Editor
- · Picasa
- · Ribbet
- · PicMonkey

For more tips and styling inspiration, visit Holly's website (www.hollybooth.com).

CHECKLIST

You've just completed another EPIC week – there ain't no stopping you now! Here's an overview of everything you've done:

- ☐ You've reviewed your Countdown to launch checklist and thought about all the things you need to do to get ready to launch

- ☐ You've read about the grown-up stuff and decided on the best legal structure for your creative business

- ☐ You've checked any other legislative requirements for starting your business where you live by looking through our resources

- ☐ You've read how it's normal to be feeling a bit scared or overwhelmed at this point, but you now know that taking action is the best way to keep those fears in check!

- ☐ You've read our top photography tips and maybe even started taking photos of your work

PREPARING TO LAUNCH

Week Five

Welcome to Week Five! By now, the end is very much in sight. We hope you're enjoying the process of building your website or marketplace shop, and are becoming excited about sharing your business with the world.

This week, we're continuing to work on getting your shop ready to launch. We'll be helping you craft an amazing About page, and write your product descriptions and shop policies. Phew! And in case that all sounds a bit too serious, we'll be finishing off with something altogether a lot more fun: some ways to start building the buzz ahead of your launch.

I'm excited, and hope you are too. Ready? Let's go!

WRITE SIZZLING PRODUCT DESCRIPTIONS

Before we get started, I'm going to explain why it's important to think about the words you use on your online shop – and wherever you talk about your business. Continue to read through the tips in this section, then it's time to add your product or service descriptions to your website or marketplace shop.

Why words matter

- Using the right language and tone helps you to connect with potential customers, reinforce your brand and transform browsers into buyers.

- Using the right keywords in and around your content helps your product and shop get seen by shoppers who are searching for the product or service you sell.

Here are some things to think about to get you writing that sizzling copy for your creative business:

Descriptive product names work best

When coming up with names and descriptions for your products and services, it's important to spend some time thinking about what customers might be searching for. The keywords you include in your product names will help potential customers find you through search engines and within online marketplace websites.

For example, let's imagine you're selling handmade lavender soap. Which of the following product names do you think customers are most likely to be searching for: 'handmade lavender soap' or 'Pam's Purple Polishing Bar'?

People are far more likely to find your products and services online if you use names that describe them literally

It can be tempting to come up with funny or creative names for your products and services, and this can be a great idea when your brand is established and you have a steady stream of returning customers. But in the early days it's all about helping people find what you have to offer, so using descriptive names is key.

Think like your dream customer

Remember how I told you that you'd be thinking about your dream customer at all times when working on your creative business? Well, writing product or service descriptions is an excellent case in point.

For example, you might be selling handmade lavender soap and trying to decide between the following names for your product:

· Handmade natural lavender soap

· Luxury aromatherapy soap

Now consider the following questions: Does your dream customer like to treat herself with products that inspire a feeling of luxury and decadence? Or does she prize natural products made by artisans with an expert knowledge of the therapeutic properties of plants?

Continue to think about all the questions your dream customer might ask, then make sure that you answer them in your product and service descriptions. What materials are your products made from? How big are they? Are they part of a matching set? Do you offer gift wrap? How long will it take for an order to arrive?

Getting yourself into the habit of thinking about your dream customer will make writing your product and service descriptions easier, I promise.

Being yourself is good for business

Being yourself really IS good for business: customers want to connect with a real person when buying from creative businesses. So when writing your product and service descriptions remember to be yourself. This is essential for engaging potential customers and giving them the confidence they need to buy.

Avoid any temptation to slip into over the top sales speak. If you're worried that you might be slipping into using a tone or style that isn't you, try using the 'friend filter'. When writing anything for your online shop, ask yourself: 'Is this what I would say if I was talking to a friend?' Of course, it's important to come across as reliable and trustworthy too, so always check your copy for typos before you hit the 'publish' button.

The art of copywriting

Remember that good copywriting is an art form, not a science. It's also something that will get better with time. As your business grows and develops, you'll be able to test different names and descriptions to see what works best. You'll also be able to improve your copywriting by reading other peoples' work, and you'll be able to refer to the great resources in this book (see Resources).

For now, just concentrate on getting your product or service descriptions ready in time for launch, and adding them to your online shop. You can keep adding and improving these as you become more experienced and receive feedback from customers further down the line.

Write an amazing About page

WORKSHEET

You'll need an About page or introduction text for your website or online shop. This is something that makes a lot of creative business owners feel frustrated and stuck, but fear not! The main thing to remember when it comes to writing your About page is to be yourself. Customers are looking to connect with a REAL PERSON when buying from a creative business owner, not some faceless nobody who writes in bland business speak.

So try not to worry about it too much. As with everything else, you can always come back and tweak your About page at a later date. For now, the important thing is to get it done, so give yourself no more than one hour to write answers to the following prompts, then come back and refine them into a paragraph or two of copy. When you're ready, you can add this copy to your online shop.

1. What do you create, offer or sell?

2. How does your product or service make people feel?

3. What techniques, processes or materials do you use – and why?

4. What makes your product or service special or different?

5. How much love, care and attention go into doing what you do?

6. What are your inspirations?

7. What do other people say about your work?

8. Where can customers find out more about you?

9. How and where can customers get in touch with you?

PREPARE YOUR SHOP POLICIES

When selling a product or service online, you'll need to provide your customers with certain information about what they can expect when dealing with you. Having clear terms and conditions is important for customers, but will serve to protect you, too. Depending on where you live, you may also be required by law to give customers certain rights when purchasing from you online, such as the right to return or cancel an order if they change their mind.

To start compiling your shop policies, you'll need to add the following information to your online shop:

- Information explaining how customers can contact you
- Your returns and cancellations policy, plus any guarantees
- A description of the product or service you're going to provide
- The payment methods you accept on your shop
- Delivery information, including how long deliveries will take to arrive
- The final price customers will pay for purchases, including the delivery cost

- Your website terms and conditions, including a privacy policy if you collect information from visitors (for example, if you have a mailing list)

Contact information

Making it easy for potential customers to find your contact details can present them with the reassurance they need to buy, so don't bury these details away! Some people won't buy from an online shop if there isn't a telephone number displayed; at the very least, you'll need to supply an email address that customers can use to get in touch with you if they have any questions.

Returns and cancellations policy

Your returns and cancellations policy should make it easy for customers to understand what to do if they want to return or cancel an order they have placed with you, or are unhappy with a service you have agreed to provide.

A good returns policy will also help to reassure customers about the quality and service you offer, and can help them gain the confidence they need to buy. Remember that when buying online, customers can't pick up an item or ask you a question face-to-face.

In some regions and countries customers will have a statutory right to return or cancel goods bought online for a certain number of days. For example, the Consumer Rights Directive introduced into the EU in 2014 states that consumers have a 14-day 'cooling off' period, as well as other rights. This may not apply to some orders, such as items made to order, or digital goods.

Before going any further, turn to the resources section (see Resources) and look up the laws that apply to selling online in your country.

Now ask yourself the following questions:

- How long will I give customers to return an item if it's unsuitable?
- Who will be responsible for paying the return postage?
- Will I offer a guarantee as well as my returns policy?
- What will I do if a customer is unhappy with a custom order?
- What steps should a customer follow to send something back to me?
- How can I make these steps for returning items really clear?

When you have decided on your returns and cancellations policy, it's important to make the information easy to locate on your website or online shop. Include it on your Terms and Conditions page, or on a separate Returns and Cancellations page if you prefer.

Terms and conditions

If you're using a marketplace shop, you'll not usually need to write your own terms and conditions: the marketplace will have their own Terms and Conditions page for their website. However, if you're setting up your own website, you'll need to have your own Terms and Conditions page.

Your terms and conditions should set out the terms of the contract any customer enters into when buying a product or service from you. And it's where you'll seek to set out what customers should expect when dealing with you, state any exclusions that apply and also set out the terms of use of your website. Other things that should appear in your terms and conditions are your cancellations and returns policy (even if you also choose to have this on a separate page), your delivery costs and payment information.

The easiest way to write your Terms and Conditions page is to buy a template online: just use Google to search for 'website terms and conditions template' or use the terms and conditions from a major retailer's website as a basis for creating your own. I'm not advocating copying, but you can certainly gain inspiration by looking at terms and conditions from larger online shops.

Privacy policy

If you're setting up your own website in the UK, USA, Canada, Australia or New Zealand, you'll need to have your own privacy policy that states which information you will collect from users, how you will use their details and how they can contact you if they want their details removed. If you're in the EU, you will also need to say which cookies are used on your website. Your website provider might be able to supply a free template, or you can purchase a privacy policy template online.

Now it's time for you to add your shop policies to your website or online shop. Work through your checklist and add the information required – remember to keep things simple, and make sure your shop policies are easy to find.

WRITE YOUR DELIVERY INFORMATION PAGE

If you're going to be selling physical products, now is the time to decide how you'll manage postage and packing, and to write your Delivery Information page. Spend some time today researching how you'll ensure your products reach your customers safely and securely, and decide how much you'll charge for shipping.

To do this, you may need to weigh or measure your products, research packaging options, visit the post office or research courier services online. You can also look at how other retailers manage their postage and packing, and see which system appeals to you. As you work on this, here are some other things to consider:

How low can you go?

Online shoppers expect their orders to be delivered in a timely fashion, in tip-top condition, without paying over the odds. Several studies have shown that high delivery charges discourage potential shoppers, and offering free shipping can be an excellent way to increase sales.

You may want to offer free shipping as a promotion on a tactical basis to boost sales, or you may even wish to consider offering free shipping all year round. If you do decide to follow this route, you'll need to make sure you account for the cost of shipping when deciding what to charge customers for your goods.

Per item or fixed cost shipping?

If you're planning to sell a range of products that are different weights and sizes, you'll need to decide whether to calculate your shipping costs on a per item basis, or whether to charge a standard delivery cost. To decide this, check what is possible through your marketplace or website provider, as some platforms are more flexible than others.

Express delivery services?

Another thing to think about is offering different delivery services. If you're planning to sell gifts, you really should consider offering an express or next-day delivery service. In my experience, this can make a significant difference to your sales, especially if you're planning to service last-minute shoppers like me!

- Will you ship overseas, or only to customers in the same country as you?
- Which postal service(s) will you use?
- How long should customers expect for their orders to arrive?
- Will you offer special delivery services, for example nominated day delivery or express shipping? And if so, what will the cut-off time be for orders?
- Will you charge a delivery cost per item, or a standard shipping fee?
- Will you offer any free shipping? And on what basis: on all orders, or only on orders above a certain amount?
- How will you ensure orders reach customers in pristine condition?

Ensure you include answers to the following questions as you write the Delivery Page for your own business!

As with all of these things, devising the perfect formula is more of an art form than a science. Just remember to take into account the cost of your packaging too, and try to keep things as easy as possible for customers to understand. When you have answered these questions, you have all the information needed to write your Delivery Information page. Well done!

START SOME DIY PROMOTION

As soon as you have ticked off everything on your checklist (see Countdown to Launch Worksheet), you'll nearly be ready to launch your creative business! Switching your website or marketplace shop to live is a very exciting step, but now it's time to start thinking about things you could do to help the sales roll in. As well as the activities you noted down in your getting the word out worksheet in Week Three (see Get the Word Out Worksheet), you might want to think about doing some extra promotional activities to ensure your business creates a splash – so here are some ideas:

Short-term promotions

To kick-start sales and help turn browsers into buyers, listed below are some offers and incentives you could consider running during your launch period. Remember that to prove effective all promotions should have an end date; exclusivity and limited availability are great sales triggers, too!

Ideas

- Free shipping
- Free gift for the first X amount of customers
- Free gift wrap
- Join mailing list and receive XYZ
- Giveaway or contest

Some things to think about:

Ensure that any short-term promotions you run fit with your brand. For example, if you're selling luxury beauty products aimed at an affluent customer discounting might not be the best strategy for you. Keep your dream customer in mind, and think about the promotions he or she would be attracted to.

- To reap the maximum value from any promotions you run, the key is to think long-term. Promotions and offers run the risk of reducing your profit in their early days, but have long-term benefits in terms of building your customer base. Which leads us on to...

- How will you keep in touch with customers after your initial launch phase? I would highly recommend that you start a mailing list and keep in touch with your customers via an email newsletter, rather than relying solely on social media. Mail Chimp is a great free service that makes it easy to build a mailing list.

Get the word out

Once you've decided on the promotions you're going to run, you'll need to think about how to let potential customers know about them. Here are some ideas to get you started, but don't feel limited to these alone! Use this opportunity to put your own creativity and enthusiasm to work in new ways!

Ideas

- Run a giveaway and encourage people to share details of this on social media sites for more chances to win.

- Email friends and family and ask them to help spread the word.

- Invite local press to interview you – remember, stories sell!

- Hold a launch party using Google Hangouts; invite friends and family to attend and give them a virtual demonstration of the wonderful products you have to offer (bubbly is optional...)

- Create a launch video and share it on YouTube.

- Create a launch party event on your Facebook page; invite friends and followers to login at a specific time and post photos of your work for them to admire (and buy!).

- Run a Pin It to Win It! competition on Pinterest, to encourage people to pin your products to their boards.

I'm sure you'll be able to think of plenty more ideas! Just try to keep an open mind and be creative. You'll soon get a feel for the types of promotions and events that resonate with your dream customer and generate the best results.

Become a PR pro

Which blogs and magazines write about other creative businesses you think your dream customer might admire? Write a list of them, then get in touch with each relevant blogger or journalist via email. Keep this correspondence brief: tell them what you're launching, why you think their readers would be interested, and supply an overview of the important details:

- When your creative business will launch

- What you'll be selling

- Where they'll be able to access your website or marketplace shop (the website address)

- How they can contact you with any questions they have

Don't forget to include a compelling image or two; ideally one or two of your work, and maybe even a nice photo of you.

CASE STUDY

★ PENNY DIXON ★

Owner of Penny Jane Designs

When did you make the jump to selling online?

I already had a basic website for the art workshops; luckily it wasn't too tricky to add items to the store. However, I soon realized that it might be difficult to get 'traffic' there. Chatting to other crafters at fairs, I quickly became aware of sites such as Etsy and Folksy, so I immersed myself in them, signing up for groups, forums and newsletters. It was also great fun doing virtual shopping in the name of research...

What have been the highlights for you since you started your business?

Definitely being invited to Downing Street for afternoon tea! It was part of the Small Business Saturday UK campaign and I got to meet so many interesting people from other businesses. The small things are highlights for me too, such as when someone leaves some lovely feedback about a purchase, or when I send an item abroad and imagine the person opening their parcel in another country.

Penny Dixon's journey from community artist to creative business owner has taken her all the way to No. 10 Downing Street! Penny lives in the UK and sells her fun and creative handmade felt accessories and upcycled designs via two marketplace shops, as well as her own website (www.pennyjanedesigns.webs.com).

When did you start Penny Jane Designs and why?

I began in 2007 while I was already a community artist teaching art and craft workshops all over the place. I'd always intended to make the change over to selling my own work as opposed to looking after everyone else all the time! My partner saw an advert for an arts festival and encouraged me to get some work together for it. I couldn't believe it when I returned from a day at the festival in profit, and I'd met so many great people!

What would your advice be to anyone else who is just starting their creative business and selling their products online?

Get involved with as much as possible. Be open to opportunities, as you never know where something will lead. Be sociable both online and in person. Last but not least: try to get the best photographs you possibly can for your products, as other people are likely to share them.

CHECKLIST

Wow – you've been super busy this week, and are nearly ready to launch! Here's what you've done:

 You've written some sizzling descriptions and added your first set of products or services to your online shop

 You've written an amazing About page to help customers connect with you

 You've taken care of some more grown-up bits, including your returns policy and terms and conditions for your shop

You've decided on which shipping and handling services you'll use, figured out how much to charge, and added the information to your online shop

 Last but not least, you've had some fun thinking how to build the buzz when your business goes live

You're doing a fantastic job, but there's no time to lose. Let's keep up the momentum as we approach the final week!

READY, STEADY, LAUNCH!

Week Six

Welcome to the final week of *From Passion to Profit: Start Your Business in 6 Weeks or Less*. At some point during the week, you'll be launching your creative business and opening the doors to your virtual shop!

This final lesson is focused on setting you up for success, and providing some guidance on what to do once your business actually goes live. So read through the material and complete the worksheet, as you'll want to regularly refer back to this long after you've finished this book.

We hope you've enjoyed this journey over the past six weeks, and are proud of what you have achieved. I know I am – you're a star! Good luck for the final week...

LAUNCH DAY

So the day has arrived... You've dotted the 'i's, crossed the 't's and you're ready to launch your website or marketplace shop! Here's a quick checklist to help you prepare for the day you open the virtual doors to your shop:

1. Run a final check through all the pages of your website or online shop. Are all the sections complete? Are there any typos or broken links?

2. If you haven't already done so, place a test order so you know what to expect and what communication your customers will receive when they buy from you.

3. When you're ready, set your website or marketplace shop to 'open'. The exact process for doing this will depend on the platform you're using, but in most cases it's as easy as just hitting a button that says 'publish'. If there's an option asking you if you'd like to make your shop visible to search engines, say 'yes'.

4. Post a link on social media sites and your blog, send an email to all your friends and family and to your email list if you have one already. Then kick off all the exciting promotion ideas you came up with last week (see Start Some DIY Promotion).

5. Do a happy dance! Then sit back down, make a cup of tea and try to relax – you've earned it.

6. Check your email regularly in case any orders come through on launch day, but try not to sit glued to your computer all day waiting for something to happen. You know what they say about a watched kettle, after all...

7. Reply to any messages you receive on social media and email anyone who you promised to get in touch with once your shop went live.

What if nobody buys anything?

If you don't receive any orders on launch day or even during the following few days, try not to become disheartened. The launch is just the beginning. Building an online business is a marathon, not a sprint. It takes consistent hard work to build a successful business, and despite what it might look like from the outside, very few business success stories happen overnight.

The trick is to keep trying new things, to keep learning, and to treat your online business as an experiment. There are no golden bullets and no guarantees. When it comes to marketing, be creative and don't be afraid of reaching out. You need to get out there and tell people about your business.

If you're genuinely excited about your products and what you have to offer the world, the chances are that other people will be, too. Be yourself, and don't feel like you have to curb your enthusiasm when you tell other people about your work.

Reach out to the community

One of the great things about selling online is that you don't have to do any of this alone. Yes, it's your business and you might be the only one running the show (for now, at least). But there's a massive community of creative business owners out there, wherever you live in the world.

There are countless seller communities, blogs and forums that provide support and advice to creative business owners online. This means you don't even need to leave the house to get some one-to-one help! Depending on where you live, there might even be local meet-ups or seller teams who gather together face-to-face. Check out the resources section (see Resources) and make a promise to yourself to connect with at least one other business owner this week.

WHAT NEXT?

Congratulations! By now, you have a real, live business. You have a website or marketplace shop, and are poised and ready to take orders from adoring customers who want and need your work!

ORDERS

Give yourself a pat on the back!

The most important thing to do now is to look at what you've achieved, and give yourself a pat on the back. You have come further in six weeks than many people do in a lifetime. You have taken decisions, confronted fears and turned ideas into actions in record time. Seriously – well done! Even if you have yet to experience the thrill of someone paying real money for something you have created, that moment will arrive. For now, just take a few moments to appreciate how far you have come.

Adopt the right mindset

Remember the goals and ambitions that you set out in Week One? Now is the time to dig out your dream business worksheet (see Imagine Your Dream Business Worksheet) and look at what you wrote on it. Does your biggest business goal seem a bit closer now your venture is actually live? Are you daring to dream big, and think about what you want to achieve? Maybe you're finding it hard to make the connection between where you are now and where you want to be?

If that is the case, don't stress. Remember that all successful businesses started where you are now: at the beginning. Launching a business is just that – a start, a launching pad. Later this week we'll be talking about planning for profit and engineering your way to growth. For now though, spend some time re-connecting with the vision you have for your business, and what you ultimately want to achieve.

Surround yourself with the right people

We've already talked about the importance of getting support from the creative community when starting your business. It's important to seek support now more than ever – but not just from anyone.

Launching a business is often seen as an invitation for friends and family to give feedback and 'constructive' criticism. Comments on your pricing, logo, website design...all these can be well meaning, but can cause fatal knocks to your confidence and self-esteem. Accept feedback graciously, but don't take it too seriously unless it comes from one of the following groups of people:

1. Somebody who fits your target customer profile

2. A peer on the same journey as you, such as another member of the creative community

3. An expert with experience that is directly relevant to what you want to do

When you receive feedback from anyone else, simply smile and say 'Thanks!' Just remember that you're building a business on your own terms, and you don't need anyone else's permission to go after your dreams.

REVIEWS

CUSTOMER LOVE

Now that your shop is open for business, you're soon going to be dealing with real life customers. How does that make you feel? Hopefully you're excited, rather than wanting to head for the hills!

Of course, while the vast majority of your customer interactions will be positive, there will undoubtedly be hiccups and problems to deal with from time to time. These are unavoidable, no matter how long you've been in business or how much experience you might have: orders get lost in the post; carefully wrapped packages become damaged in transit; birthday presents arrive late.

These problems might not always be your fault, but your customers will be looking to you to put things right. So here are a few hints and tips to help you minimize the risk of customer service issues cropping up, and some ideas to help you deal with them effectively when they do:

Aim to under promise and over deliver

When it comes to setting customer expectations with regards to turnaround times for orders, always try to under promise and over deliver. If it usually takes an average of three days for you to deliver an order or to complete a service, consider telling customers to expect delivery within seven days. Not only does this mean your customers will be surprised and delighted when their order arrives early, but also you'll save yourself time answering those 'Where is my order?' emails.

Plan ahead for holidays and special events

If you're running your business on your own, there are going to be times when you're not going to be able to handle orders as quickly as you might usually like. For example, if you're going away or are busy during the school holidays.

To avoid potential customer service problems, plan ahead. Unless you have someone to cover for you, it's a good idea to notify customers in advance. Some ways you could do this might include putting a notice on your shop, posting on your Facebook page, or sending an email. It's better to tell your customers too many times rather than risk them not noticing, and being disappointed when an order fails to arrive.

If you're selling on Etsy or another marketplace shop, you may be able to switch your shop into 'holiday' mode. This means customers will see a message saying you are away, and that they will not be able to place an order. Just don't forget to switch your shop back to 'off holiday' mode when you get back to your business!

Respond swiftly to negative feedback

Instead of becoming defensive if you receive negative feedback, try to turn each incident into an opportunity for some positive customer interaction. Maybe you can't convince a customer to like a necklace that she has decided to return, but you can leave her feeling that you're a great seller to deal with and a shop she may come back to again.

While it's tempting to let complaints or other negative emails linger in your inbox, don't. Respond to them quickly and politely, and try to see things from your customer's point of view. If a customer is angry or upset, try asking her how she would like to see the situation resolved.

This can really take the heat out of the situation, as the customer understands that you're willing to see things from his or her point of view. In our experience, customers often want less than you would have been willing to give, which makes this situation an eventual win-win!

And finally...

As difficult as it might be, try not to let customer service incidents get you down if they do crop up. Don't take things personally, and see what you can learn from the situation. Perhaps there is something you could do to try and avoid the same problem happening again, such as improving your product descriptions or including clearer terms and conditions on your website? Or perhaps there really is nothing more you could have done. In which case, remind yourself of all the happy customers who are delighted with everything you've done for them, take a deep breath, smile – and remember that tomorrow is another day.

Plan for profit

WORKSHEET

As I said right at the beginning of this book, building a thriving business takes time, energy and commitment. You've already done a lot of the hard work, and taken the decisions that will set you up for success. Great! To build on this foundation and to create a profitable business, you'll need to keep a focus on the activities that will make the biggest difference to your business. The easiest way to ensure you do this is by creating (and sticking to) a plan.

Why is planning so important?

Because without a plan, a goal is just a wish. Without knowing step-by-step what we need to do to meet our goals, we risk becoming overwhelmed and spending our time on the wrong things. Or worse still, not taking any action at all!

So spend some time now thinking about what actions you'll take to get your business moving in the right direction to bring in customers and sales. You might want to plan three months ahead, six months ahead or just one month at a time.

You decide what you're most comfortable with then start working from there. You can use this worksheet to help you, a year planner, or you can create a system of your own. The key is to find something that works for you, that you'll be happy using every day.

You've already created a marketing plan in Week Three (see Get the Word Out Worksheet). You've also created an overall vision and strategy for your business in Week One (see Imagine Your Dream Business Worksheet). Now it's time to break these bigger goals and strategies down into an action plan to ensure you keep moving forward, and to plan for profit.

My goal this year is to ....

Month:

Major projects	I'm focusing on this because.....	To make sure this happens I will....

WORKSHEET

CASE STUDY

BECKY DOGGETT & OWEN BIRKBY

Founders of Handmade Nation

Becky Doggett and Owen Birkby are the founders of Handmade Nation (www.handmade-nation.com), a website and community for handmade sellers. Thousands of creative business owners join in their #HandmadeHour online networking sessions each week (Twitter.com/HandmadeHour).

How did the idea for #HandmadeHour come about?

The first ever #HandmadeHour was in May 2013. We wanted to give the craft community an opportunity to come together to network, showcase their talents, and find clients and support services. There were around 300 tweets altogether in the first ever #HandmadeHour, and Owen was able to retweet every photo! Now we have thousands it's a little more difficult to keep up...

How can online networking events such as #HandmadeHour help creative business owners, especially newcomers?

#HandmadeHour is a fantastic platform for creative businesses to showcase their products, talk to other creative business owners, share ideas and reach potential customers. During the two-hour weekly networking slot, on average over TWO MILLION people across the world see tweets containing the #HandmadeHour hashtag. There is simply no other way to get that kind of exposure, for free, in such a short space of time!

It's a lot more than just showing off your products though. Through #HandmadeHour we have managed to create an ever-growing community of like-minded individuals who enjoy talking to one another. If you have a question or are stuck for ideas, the chances are there will be someone who has the answer or is willing to help. From start-ups to businesses that have been running for ten years or more, there is knowledge and experience from all levels to offer help and support. #HandmadeHour is very welcoming and everyone wants to help each other to succeed.

#TWITTER

What advice would you give to someone who is just starting out as a creative business owner, or trying to decide what business to start?

Do something you love! Running your own business requires a lot of hours, so if you don't love what you are doing then you won't see it through. Once you've started your business, you need to be getting the word out and showing people what you do. So whether it's through social media using sessions, such as #HandmadeHour, blogging or listing your products on a marketplace, find a way to get yourself out there and find an audience.

Remember there is nothing wrong with asking for advice. Everyone started from nothing and we all learned from our mistakes as we went along.

What's the proudest moment you've had since starting #HandmadeHour?

Our first proudest moment was when #HandmadeHour trended at number 1 on Twitter in the UK. The second is when, from the success of #HandmadeHour, we got a huge demand to launch networking events to better suit different time zones, and so on 23 April 2014 at 7pm EDT #HandmadeHourUSA was born – and was a huge success!

CHECKLIST

You've done it! This week has just about brought you to the end of our journey together, and your creative business is officially OPEN.

- [ ] You've launched your online shop

- [ ] You've given yourself a well-deserved pat on the back

- [ ] You've looked up some sources of ongoing help and support

- [ ] You've thought about how you'll handle customer services for your shop

- [ ] And you've created your planning for profit business action plan

I'm so proud of you. Well done!

★ GOODBYE ★

Now you've reached the end of this book, and launched your creative business to the world. I hope you're very proud of everything you've achieved. I've been rooting for you over the past six weeks, and I hope you've felt my enthusiasm and energy transcend the barriers of space and time...

Of course, this is just the start. Launching your website or online shop is where the real excitement begins! As I've already said – you're going to need to put some ongoing effort into promoting your business, and it will take some time to build up. But I know you've got it in you, and it's going to be great.

Remember to look through the following resources, as you'll find plenty of additional sources of help and advice that will keep you company on your journey as a creative entrepreneur. Otherwise, please keep in touch with me on social media and let me know how you get on. Wishing you all the luck in the world!

You really have done something amazing, and are at the beginning of a really exciting journey!

Remember, keep trying new things, stay positive and have fun!

 www.twitter.com/clairiel

tfi.monday.com

 www.facebook.com/handmadehorizons

★ RESOURCES ★

Legal and government resources

Look at these official resources for the most up-to-date advice on legislation and regulations when starting your business. In these you'll find information on business structures, how to register your business, and the relevant laws and rules that apply when selling products and services online.

USA

Selling online: www.business.ftc.gov
Setting up a business and registering your name: www.sba.gov
Tax and record keeping: www.irs.gov
www.uspto.gov

UK

All aspects of starting a business, including regulations for selling online and trademarks: www.gov.uk/business
Tax and record keeping, including registering for self-assessment: www.hmrc.gov.uk

Australia

Business start-up advice: www.ato.gov.au
Apply for Australian Business Number: abr.gov.aus
Search for and register trademarks: www.ipaustralia.gov.au
Selling online: www.digitalbusiness.gov.au

New Zealand

Business start-up advice: www.business.govt.nz
Tax and record keeping: www.ird.govt.nz
Search for and register trademarks: www.iponz.govt.nz

Canada

Business start-up advice, including registering your business and selling online: www.canadabusiness.ca
Register your business: www.cra-arc.gc.ca

South Africa

Advice on all aspects of starting and growing a business http://southafrica.smetoolkit.org/sa/en

Blogs and creative communities

Oh My! Handmade Goodness: ohmyhandmade.com
Handmade Success: handmadesuccess.com
UK Handmade: ukhandmade.co.uk
BlogAndBuySale: www.blogandbuysale.com
Poppytalk Handmade: www.poppytalk.com
Papernstitch: www.papernstitchblog.com
Handmade Hour (on Twitter): use #HandmadeHour or #HandmadeHourUSA
Folksy: blog.folksy.com

Business training and advice

Although some of these organizations offer paid-for training, they also offer lots of free advice via their websites and blogs. Sign up for their email digests to receive regular advice and to pick up tips from other creative business owners.

IdeasTap: www.ideastap.com
The Abundant Artist: theabundantartist.com
Flourish & Thrive Academy: www.flourishthriveacademy.com/blog
Design Trust Biz Ladies: www.designsponge.com/category/biz-ladies
The Design Trust: www.thedesigntrust.co.uk
Maker's Nation: www.makersnation.org
Enterprise Nation: www.enterprisenation.com
Handmade Horizons: www.handmadehorizons.com
School for Creative Startups: www.schoolforcreativestartups.com
Etsy blog: blog.etsy.com
Copyblogger: www.copyblogger.com/blog
Handmade Success: www.handmadesuccess.com
Foodpreneurs: www.blog.yumbles.com

★ ABOUT THE AUTHOR ★

Claire Hughes is an online retail expert, a marketing geek and a third generation entrepreneur. Graduating with a journalism degree at the height of the dot-com boom, Claire decided the explosion of e-commerce was too exciting to ignore and dived right in. After starting her online marketing career in London, Claire spent many years helping big brands like AOL, McAfee and BT sell their products and services online, before starting her own business as a freelance marketing consultant and copywriter in 2009.

Since then Claire has helped hundreds of business owners start and grow a successful online business, via both Handmade Horizons, a training company for handmade sellers she co-founded in 2012, and her latest project, TFI Monday! Her advice has been featured on websites including Handmade Success, The Design Trust and the Folksy blog. She is a regular instructor for the Creative University and loves nothing more than helping talented, passionate people make things happen online.

Claire now lives in a small village in North Wales sandwiched between the mountains and sea, with her partner, her dog and two young kids. She tweets at @clairiel and blogs at tfimonday.com.

★ ACKNOWLEDGMENTS ★

With huge thanks to my family, Mollie, the Handmade Horizons community and all the lovely ladies who contributed to this book. Thanks so much; I couldn't have done this without you.

Big respect and thanks also to all the amazing people whose words have inspired and guided me in my own journey over the past few years. In no particular order: Sir Richard Branson, Chris Guillebeau, Chis Brogan, John Williams, Marie Forleo, Seth Godin, James Altucher, Jennifer Louden and SARK. Thanks for doing what you do.

★ INDEX ★

A DAVID & CHARLES BOOK
© F&W Media International, Ltd 2014

David & Charles is an imprint of F&W Media International, Ltd
Brunel House, Forde Close, Newton Abbot, TQ12 4PU, UK

F&W Media International, Ltd is a subsidiary of F+W Media, Inc
10151 Carver Road, Suite #200, Blue Ash, OH 45242, USA

First published in the UK and USA in 2014

A catalogue record for this book is available from the British Library.

ISBN-13: 978-1-4463-0501-0 paperback
ISBN-10: 1-4463-0501-5 paperback

ISBN-13: 978-1-4463-6921-0 PDF
ISBN-10: 1-4463-6921-8 PDF

ISBN-13: 978-1-4463-6920-3 EPUB
ISBN-10: 1-4463-6920-X EPUB

Printed in Slovenia by GPS Group for:
F&W Media International, Ltd
Brunel House, Forde Close, Newton Abbot, TQ12 4PU, UK

10 9 8 7 6 5 4 3 2 1

Acquisitions Editor: Ame Verso
Editors: Matthew Hutchings and Emma Gardner
Project Editor: Freya Dangerfield
Designer: Jenny Stanley
Production Manager: Beverley Richardson

F+W Media publishes high quality books on a wide range of subjects.
For more great book ideas visit: **www.stitchcraftcreate.co.uk**